ACTOR'S CHOICE:
Monologues for Men

ACTOR'S CHOICE:

Monologues for Men

Edited by Erin Detrick

New York, NY

Actor's Choice: Monologues for Men is published by Playscripts, Inc., 325 West 38th Street, Suite 305, New York, New York, 10018, www.playscripts.com

Cover design by Another Limited Rebellion
Text design and layout by Jason Pizzarello

First Edition: April 2008
10 9 8 7 6 5 4 3 2 1

Editor's Note: In some of the monologues in this book, dialogue or stage directions from the play may have been removed for clarity's sake.

Library of Congress Cataloging-in-Publication Data

Actor's choice : monologues for men / edited by Erin Detrick.
    p. cm.
Summary: "Collection of monologues from the Playscripts, Inc. catalog of plays, representing a variety of American playwrights. The source material for each monologue may be found on the Playscripts website, where nearly the entire text of every play can be read for free. Intended for male actors"--Provided by publisher.
    ISBN-13: 978-0-9709046-5-2 (pbk.)
    1. Monologues. 2. Acting. 3. American drama--20th century. 4. Men--Drama. I. Detrick, Erin, 1981-
    PN2080A2868 2008
    808.82'45--dc22
                        2007050163

Acknowledgments

First and foremost, this book was made possible by all of the exceptionally talented playwrights who so generously allowed us to include their work. We are deeply appreciative.

Special thanks are due to Jason Pizzarello, Doug Briggs, and Devin McKnight for their monumental contributions to the creation of this book. Thanks also to Noah Scalin, Terry Nemeth, and Arthur Stanley.

Table of Contents

INTRODUCTION

Finding the perfect monologue can be a complicated task. You need a strong, juicy piece of material that will highlight your talents—preferably a piece that hasn't been seen thousands of times already. Furthermore, to fully understand the context of your monologue, you need the play itself at your fingertips to help you prepare. Often that play is impossible to track down. That's where *Actor's Choice* comes in.

We at Playscripts, Inc. have long looked forward to creating a book of monologues drawn from the 1000+ plays we publish. There's a wealth of engaging, dynamic monologues found within those plays—and we're thrilled to make many of them available to you now.

But here's what makes *Actor's Choice* truly unique: For every monologue, you have the option of reading up to 90% of the play it comes from, all from one source, and all for free. Simply visit the Playscripts, Inc. website at *www.playscripts.com*. No longer do you have to waste time searching for a script— the work's already done for you.

On behalf of all the exceptional playwrights represented in this book, we hope that you enjoy these monologues, and that you get the part!

HOW TO USE THIS BOOK

Every monologue in this book is preceded by a brief description that introduces the context. If you'd like to read the play itself, we've made the process simple:

o   Go to the Playscripts, Inc. website: **www.playscripts.com**

o   Run a search for the play title.

o   Click the *Read Sample* link and read away.

o   If you'd like to read the entire play, you may order a book at any time from the Playscripts, Inc. website.

FOREWORD

Confessions of a Broadway Casting Director

I was a year out of college when I went on my first audition in New York City. A friend of mine had left school after getting cast in a national tour, and when one of his fellow actors dropped out, he got me an audition to replace her. I was living in Virginia at the time, so I quickly planned a trip to the big city. I still remember driving over the Verrazano Bridge, nervous with anticipation, and heading to my friend's apartment in Queens. I had picked an outfit, rested my voice, and agonized over which song I should sing. The next day at the audition I walked into the room and sang my song, following all the audition rules I'd learned in college. When I finished I turned expectantly to the casting director. She looked down at my headshot, and then back at me with a slightly confused look and said, "So, who do you—where did...you...come from?" When I explained that my friend was in the tour, it was as if a light went on in her head. She nodded knowingly; my appearance in the casting call suddenly made sense. Even with my lack of big city audition experience, I knew this was not a good sign. I had clearly made some rookie mistakes, I didn't get the part, and I left New York feeling I had blown my big chance.

I moved to New York City shortly thereafter and only lasted a year before I gave up acting. Fortunately, I found another great vocation—on the other side of the table as a casting director. If I knew then what I know now, that first audition would have gone a lot differently.

I truly believe that actors have one of the hardest jobs around. Just look at the audition situation alone—actors have to be charming but not arrogant, vulnerable but not needy, friendly but not so friendly that the people on the other side of the table start to get scared. They have to be interesting, brilliant, moving, memorable, and right for the part. Often all in three minutes or less.

Some audition tips are obvious. Then again, I've still seen each of the following scenarios on several occasions, so perhaps these tips bear repeating...

o Don't stand too close to the person behind the table. Firstly because it's an invasion of personal space, and secondly because a little distance helps us with perspective.

o If there is a reader present for your audition, please don't excessively touch or molest them. Unfortunately, I've seen it happen often and it's uncomfortable for everyone.

o If your audition involves reading a scene, don't worry about memorizing lines unless you've been asked to. I'd much rather watch an actor refer to pages and be in the moment, than watch them mentally panic over what the next line is.

o Always second-guess the use of props, and the amount of the audition you spend lying on, crawling across, rolling around on, or throwing yourself to the floor. You don't have to tell me which special skills on your resume make you really right for this and how much you want this part. I know you want this part, as I assume you wouldn't be here if you didn't.

o And finally, unless we know each other, it's probably best to leave your personal life out of the audition room. I've had people tell me about everything from brain tumors to painful divorces. And while I'd happily hear about your life over a cup of coffee, the audition room is not the right forum for it.

What many actors don't know is that the people on the other side of the table are actually on your side. We desperately want you to be our answer. We want you to be brilliant just as badly as you want to be brilliant. The best auditions I've seen have been when actors come in the room simply as themselves. Don't waste your energy trying to figure out who or what you think we want you to be. Be who you are. It's always more interesting. Because as much as this is going to sound like your mother talking, there is no one out there like you. No one brings exactly the same things to a scene or monologue that you do. So find out what it is that you are able to relate to in a character and explore it. And when you do, figure out where the vulnerability is. In every audition, you've got to create a compelling character. Finding the vulnerability means that I get to see exactly what that character is really feeling, even if it's ugly or embarrassing. And that is always fascinating to watch.

The monologues in this book do half of the work for you. They are fresh, truthful, and interesting, not to mention brand-new material (which means I won't be comparing you to the girl/guy who used your same monologue five people ago). If you can deliver a monologue that is genuine, natural, and has vulnerability to it, even if you're not right for whatever I might be casting that day, I will put you in my "Remember Them" file and keep you in mind for other opportunities down the road. In the long run, so much of casting has to do with tiny details that are beyond your control. So do yourself a favor. Show up, give a truthful performance, and let the rest go. You are enough.

Again, if only I had known that, who knows how my first audition in New York would have turned out...!

Kate Schwabe
Associate Casting Director, Jim Carnahan Casting
Roundabout Theatre Company, New York City

ACT A LADY

Jordan Harrison

True, who is playing a woman in his town's local play, ponders the transformation he is being asked to undergo.

TRUE. Back in the merchant marines, I remember a fella who put two coconuts on his chest and called that a lady. Entered himself in the cadet talent show, strummed on a banjo missing a string and sang "*Under the mango tree...*" He didn't look pretty, no, far from, with a big mouth drawn on like the south sea natives, it weren't half pretty. But I remember everybody leaned forward in their chairs, like they watched it sorta *different* because of how he looked. Guess it had the interest of something uncommon. Like a magnet—it's hard to explain. He put on those two coconuts and suddenly everyone with their eyes bigger than if he were a hunderd-percent lady swishing in that grass skirt. I got no problem wearing a dress, 'less it pinches. I just don't know if I call it *art*. I know: what right I got to judge? I tan I'm a tanner I tan things I tan. But one time my partner Knox and I stuffed two otters right outta the Stick River and mounted them like you couldn't hardly tell they weren't alive. Like we put the life back in them 'cause of how we posed them. Nobody could say that wasn't something to see. I guess I never thoughta myself as something to see. But if that Zina wants a tanner for a Countess, I'll do my best to make 'em lean forward.

ALOHA, SAY THE PRETTY GIRLS

Naomi Iizuka

Derek has cast his roommate's dog into oblivion. He wonders about the redemptive power of "aloha."

DEREK. ok, aloha. i've been thinking about this. aloha means good-bye, but it also means hello. it actually means a lot of things. it's all about how you say it. you could say it as you're going, and the plane's about to take off, and you're waving, and you could just say aloha, just let one fly, and if you were to say aloha like that, with the wave and everything else, i think everyone would be pretty clear about your meaning, but now let's say you're arriving here, you know, in hawaii, and the airplane touches down, and the door opens, and suddenly you get a whiff of that air, do you know what i'm talking about? warm and moist and all smelling of plumeria, which is like a kind of orchid, i guess, and you're making your way down the little metal staircase, and the light is so bright, it's blinding, and you're reeling from the smell of orchid, it's like the whole world is one big, bright orchid somebody just shoved in your face, and you are so overwhelmed, you don't even know what to do with yourself, and so what you do is you trip, you don't mean to, but you do, you just kinda fall, you fall down, and before you know it, you're flat on your back on the tarmac, and this pretty girl is standing over you, and maybe she's wearing a grass skirt, or maybe not, but it doesn't really matter 'cause the key detail, alright, is that around her neck, she's wearing all these leis, and before you know it, she's slipping one of her leis over your head, and you're overcome with this smell of orchid, and she's leaning real close, and whispering in your ear: aloha. she says, aloha. and i don't think it means good-bye in this situation. i think it means something else.

Aloha, Say the Pretty Girls

Naomi Iizuka

Richard, who has a net worth of 76 million dollars, worries about where he may be heading.

RICHARD. o my lord, where to begin? i was in the airport, and i was very late, i was very late, and the thing that slowly began to dawn on me was that i was so late, i was never going to get where i was going, it just wasn't going to happen, and i should've just given up, i should've just gone with the flow, but i don't know how to do that, because that's not who i am, because i haven't evolved, i haven't evolved to that point where i can look at my whole life imploding before my eyes, and just say, que sera sera, or whatever it is people say, because this is not about missed connections, this is not about air travel, because in a larger sense, i'm going to miss my flight, and then i'm going to be on stand by, i'm just going to be standing by, or maybe i'm going to be bumped, i'm just going to be bumped, and then i'm going to be stuck in this airport for the rest of all eternity like some suitcase nobody ever claims, one of those sorry, old samsonites that just keeps going round and round on the carousel, all dented and coming apart at the seams, and the clothes are coming out every which way, and there's some duct tape maybe wrapped around the middle, and maybe a little string, and the bag is a mess, it's just a mess, and all you can think is: how did this bag get to be this way? whose bag is this, and where is this person now? what happened to them? did something bad happen to them?

ASYLUM

Keith Aisner

After collapsing from exhaustion during his first date with Angela, Gary explains to her his quest for happiness through dreams he can control, and why he has good reason to fear for his sanity.

GARY. All right. Well. I've learned how to control my dreams and I'm using them to try and figure myself out…figure out how to be happy. And it's worked, you know…I think I'm really close to something. But the deeper I get the more time I spend dreaming and the harder it is to know when I'm awake. And now, just recently…like tonight…I think I might be getting lost.

My mother's in an institution. Actually, she was about the age I am now when she went in. She's been there for about 20 years. When I was six she was diagnosed with schizophrenia…which can be hereditary. My brother Frank remembers when she was more…level. She started losing it right after I was born so she was never normal to me. My dad was shattered. After he finally had her admitted he put up with us until I left home. I had a guinea pig. He was named Green Lantern. I think I was seven, and one of my friends had these really cool fish you could see through. So, of course, I wanted a fish too, but my father said Green Lantern was all I could handle. But I kept bugging them. Especially my mom, because I knew she was more likely to buy me something on the spur of the moment. And one day I came home and she was really excited, and she told me to go look in my room. And right there, next to my bed, with a big blue bow around the rim, was a fish bowl full of water. And Green Lantern was in it, tied to a rock, floating near the bottom. She said she did it so he could swim better. She tied him to the rock 'cause he kept trying to get out.

(Beat.)

I really liked that guinea pig. We spent a lot of time together. But I never blamed my mother for drowning him. Even back then I knew Green Lantern was the victim of some outside force that kind of haunted my mother's body and made her do strange things. A couple months after that she was in an institution.

ATWATER: FIXIN' TO DIE

Robert Myers

Political adviser Lee Atwater visits President Ronald Reagan to brief him on the significance for American politics of MTV, a new, all-music television network.

LEE. Good evening, Mr. President. *(Pause.)* I didn't realize it was so late. *(Pause.)* No sir, I meant you're ready for bed, sir. *(Pause.)* That's one advantage of being the chief executive. You can wear whatever you damn well please. *(Pause.)* They look comfortable. Are they silk? *(Pause.)* No, I've never been to Bloomingdale's. How is Mrs. Reagan? *(Pause.)* I noticed the workmen downstairs. She's obviously got an eye for decorating. *(Pause.)* That business about the china was bullshit, if you'll pardon my French, sir. I guess they expected you and the first lady to give state dinners on paper plates. That was just the media trying to make the most out of the recession. *(Pause.)* No, I was talking about the slowdown in '82, the dip in the economy. *(Rapidly changing the subject:)* The reason I'm here is I asked Deaver and Ailes if I might give you a quick briefing to get you up to speed on some of the more recent developments in the media. I brought a tape with me I want you to look at. *(Referring to the TV screen:)* This is a fellow named John Cougar Mellencamp. It's a music video from MTV. Do you know what that is? *(Pause.)* There was an article in *Reader's Digest?* Really. No, I missed that. *(Pause.)* What you're looking at is a whole new way of delivering information. Fast, slick, exciting, lots of quick cuts, sophisticated choreography. *(Pause.)* Exactly. *(Chuckling and nodding, as though amazed by Reagan's immediate understanding of the briefing:)* It IS sort of like an MGM musical in fast motion. This is what the kids are watching these days. MTV is the fastest growing network in America, and the audience is mostly young, white, male, 18 to 25. It's the voters we'll need in November, the swing voters. The so-called

Reagan Democrats. This is how they process information. Visually. They're the generation that grew up with TV. They want constant color, constant excitement. They want it all spelled out. Their attention span is very short. *(Pause.)* I agree. They ARE a natural Republican constituency. I just think there's a perception out there created by the media that Republicans don't know how to have fun. That's one reason I wanted you to see this. Because of your background in the industry. Your ability to ad-lib. You're very quick on your feet, very adaptable and I wanted you to know that we'll be framing your message with this group in mind.

It's been a long day for me too, sir. *(Pause, looks at his watch.)* Seven-thirty? Already? I had no idea.

Yes, sir. If I see your daughter Patty, I will tell her to lighten up.

ATWATER: FIXIN' TO DIE

Robert Myers

Political adviser Lee Atwater, who is dying of brain cancer, tries to justify the harsh campaign tactics he employed in the recent presidential election and tries to convince his opponents and himself that he is not a racist.

LEE. I always thought whatever I was really going to do with my life wouldn't begin until I turned forty. That everything that came before, everything I was living, was just a prelude, a preparation. I was expecting a test, or maybe it was expecting me, but no one expects this and whatever you may think of me I don't deserve it. No one does. I could tell you how much it's hurt Sally and the girls, how bad I feel that they treat me like someone they recognize from TV. I had a baby girl two months before my birthday, but I'm too weak to hold her and she starts crying when she sees me. I think my face like this frightens her. My fingers are so swollen I'll probably never play the guitar again, and I know I'll never be able to run. The President called again yesterday to ask how I was doing, and today I'm proud and happy, but yesterday, all the time we were talking, I couldn't remember who the President was. I fought the good fight and when I finally figured out it was all over, I asked my aides to research all the religions so I could try to figure out what I believe. I'm a Christian now, and I read the Bible everyday. Sometimes when I try to go to sleep I lay awake all night I'm so scared I won't wake up, and I pray or I think about my family or my little brother Joe. I wrote a letter to Dukakis… I dictated it. I can't hold a pen anymore…and I asked him to do a sick a man a favor, to forgive me. I'm truly sorry about a lot of things I did, especially saying I'd made Willie Horton Dukakis's running mate, because it makes me sound like a racist, which I'm not. Believe me, when you reach this point you don't hate anyone. I mean that. I love everybody. Honestly. Honestly.

CARSON MCCULLERS
(HISTORICALLY INACCURATE)

Sarah Schulman

Reeves, husband of playwright Carson McCullers, is acceding to Carson's demand for a guided sexual fantasy. What he reveals, however, is his own romantic desire for tenderness and intimacy. Not what she had in mind.

REEVES. Oh, *(Unsure:)* all right. Let's see… You mean like… Ok, we're in a cinema, in a small town. Back by Charleston. Hardly anyone is in the theater. We're watching a funny, dumb romantic comedy, it's as though we are alone. Then you put your arm around me in the theater and start stroking my head, my neck, my shoulders. Then you reach over and unbutton my shirt, stroke the hair on my chest. All the love in your heart is open to me and coming at me and I'm getting very aroused, very. I'm longing for you and you're giving me everything in your arms and in your two hands, which are now molesting me. Holding me between my thighs. You whisper in my ear "Reeves, I love you." We walk out of the theater, excited, beaming. It is a beautiful night. Warm and cool at the same time. Down at the pier, the longshoremen on the night shift are loading and unloading their ships, sailors strolling, playing cards and smoking. We come to an old rotting pier and crawl over the no trespass sign, out onto the thick, spare beams over the shinning water, all that activity on the boats behind us, and I unbutton your blouse and take the full weight of your breasts in my mouth, press myself against you, Carson and we're so filled with love.

CLAWFOOT
AND HOT TUB INTERVIEWS

Werner Trieschmann

The overenthusiastic do-it-yourselfer Jake is trying to convince Olivia, who he has never met, that he's the right man to own her clawfoot bathtub and for the rest of her natural life.

JAKE. Sure, some *calls*. I'm here. In the flesh. I can pull it out myself. Let me lift up this end. No prob. I'm strong that way. I don't go to the doctor. I do not mess with those blood suckers. All I own is a box of band aids and some rubbing alcohol. One time I sliced open my arm on this sheet metal. Got a nasty cut right down to the muscle. My supervisor begged me to go to the emergency room. Instead I went home, had some shots of tequila and sewed it up myself. I'm independent, do-it-yourself guy. You're like me. Yeah, I've seen you out. I've seen you at Puritan Foods, getting those Soups for One. You bought a hammer there. Was it last week? Yeah. Not the place to buy tools, but I didn't say anything. I've seen you by feminine stuff at the pharmacy. And those pills, too. I figure Valium or Zoloft. Am I right? No, I'm not *stalkin'* you. I got time on my hands. With the hammer, I figured you were hanging a picture of a boat. One of those catamarans in the Caribbean. I had fun thinking about how you were going to hang that picture and bang your thumb. I thought about how I should be doing it.

You know you got one of the worse houses in Pleasant Acres. Your eves are a joke. I could hang pictures, install a water heater, replaster your walls, regrout your tub, restain your furniture, insulate your attic and weather strip your door frames. I'd make this house a vault and you won't need to turn on the heater. You could walk naked in the middle of winter. You got a nail that's come up right here *(Showing with his foot.)* and another one here. You've got particle board under here. I can rip that up and put a layer of underlayman and then a new floor. It'll hold up 'til our grandkids are goin' ape crazy on it. Last for centuries. That's what's missing. Permanence. And me.

COURT-MARTIAL AT FORT DEVENS

Jeffrey Sweet

Kimball is a US Colonel supervising a hospital during World War II. He defends his choice to demote a group of black W.A.C. nurses to orderlies.

KIMBALL. Me, I'm from a little town on the coast of Maine. My bet is on this base we've got people here from just about every corner of every state in the country. Now, one of the reasons we've got all these different states—back when this country was founded the people in each of these places thought of themselves as distinct. And they wanted to keep it that way. Robert E. Lee, for instance. The Civil War was approaching, Lincoln offered him the command of the Union army. Did you know that? He could have commanded the Union army. Lee turned it down. He thought of himself as a Virginian more than as an American. And that's what he fought for, Virginia. Most of the men in this camp—before they joined the army—most of them had never been more than twenty-five miles from the place of their birth. That's been their world. They're like Lee—they're Virginians, or Minnesotans or Texans. They don't have the *experience* of being Americans. Who they are is mostly what their home is. Whatever state, whatever town. And for a lot of the boys here, those towns are in the South. They come here to Massachusetts, they bring the South with them. This base is filled with boys, what they know of the colored and how to deal with them is how they've been brought up. And I don't have time to re-educate them to see things as Mrs. Roosevelt does. And that's leaving aside whether *I* see things as Mrs. Roosevelt does. I'm not going to put together folks who have a historic dislike and mistrust of each other any more than I have to. I have a hospital to run, and I'm going to avoid disruption and upset as much as I can.

COURT-MARTIAL AT FORT DEVENS

Jeffrey Sweet

Hughes, an Episcopalian priest, preaches against an army honeycombed with prejudice.

HUGHES. When they enlisted, these young women were told that they would be assigned duties commensurate with their training and experience. But, having been sworn into the Army, they were assigned the traditional, stereotyped occupation of the Negro as a carrier of slops and a scrubber of floors. As ethical beings they rebelled. They refused to go back to work.

Now, I will grant you that these young women had a fair trial according to the rules. You cannot strike in the Army. It is illegal. On the purely technical and legal grounds on which the case was tried, they had no case. The court was concerned only with the legality, not the morality of the case.

But we here—*we* look beyond the technically legal. We examine the *ethics* of the case. We search for the grievances which produced this insubordination. And the answer is that the Army of the United States is honeycombed with prejudice, and no moral being can tolerate that. No army can ignore morals and keep up morale. So it was with reason that these young women broke the rules. Their action was a refusal to further countenance an insult. If they are rebels against "law and order,"—or what passes for law and order—so were Washington and Jefferson and Madison and the members of the Boston Tea Party.

"I will take death," said Private Johnnie Mae Malone. Is this not what every American boy, Negro or white, who faces a German bullet is saying today? "We will take death rather than acknowledge that Nazis are the masters and we are the slaves." The days of white supremacy—which is no different from the Nazi race doctrine which we now fight—are numbered.

Now the rest of us must do our part. We have been too afraid heretofore. We play safe; we give in to segregation, and sometimes even segregate ourselves because we do not want to be insulted. But somebody must make the test. These young women—hardly out of their teens—were willing to die. What are *we* prepared to do? The world belongs to men and women of pioneer spirit; men and women not afraid to risk something to advance the cause of their people. Only *they* know the joy of rising again with a great resurrection.

DEAD WAIT

Carson Kreitzer

Ron has recently landed in limbo. He hasn't really accepted his death yet. An ordinary night, a long shift waiting tables, stopping by Nicole Simpson's Brentwood home to drop off a pair of glasses that were left at the restaurant—then whammo. Game over. Not fair at all.

RON. I have, had, this collection of Zippo lighters. Y'know? Only one I have left is the one that was in my pocket. When, Y'know. My sister Kim gave me this one. See, it's uh, it's Jayne Mansfield. And it flips up at, you know, heh, her head. Her head comes off.

(Flicks the lighter several times.)

The whole thing's just shitfucked. Fucking shit. Can't stop THINKING. I coulda been a STAR after this. I coulda USED it. There's no such thing as Bad Publicity. Know what I mean? Kato couldn't handle it. I coulda handled it. Been waiting all my life for an opportunity like this. I coulda played the media like my own personal violin section. And I mean ALL the media—TV, video, audio, radio, docudrama re-enactments. AMERICA'S MOST WANTED. ME! Everybody woulda wanted a piece. Wanted me for guest shots. I woulda had my own SHOW by now. Star witness at the Trial. *Purveyor* of Justice. Criminal, Civil. That's a nice thought, huh? Civil Justice. Nice, civil Justice. cos I gotta say that was some CRIMINAL JUSTICE first time around. wouldn't a happened like that if I coulda testified. If I coulda testified…on TELEVISION. The American People rapt before the screen, tuning in everywhere, a perfect Hundred Share.

Yeah, I coulda done it Right. Then I'd have a…have a…Crime show, or a Private Detective show, in the great LA tradition. Philip Marlowe. Nicholson in Chinatown.

But not old timey, you know, HIP. A HIP, NEW Private Eye show. Every week, for millions of viewers, I'd hop in the sack with some gorgeous bimbo and solve a crime. People will come to ME because everyone knows the LAPD can't be trusted. Especially black people, right? So I'd get to fuck these gorgeous black chicks while solving their crimes and the LAPD would rough me up... Jumped in the Parking Lot. BAM! POW! Yeah, the cops'd hate me because I'm on the side of Right and Justice. And people would know they could come to ME because I'd given the crucial evidence. I'd been STAR WITNESS at the BIG FUCKING FAMOUS TRIAL.

Shit.

Dead White Males:
A Year in the Trenches of Teaching

William Missouri Downs

Principal Pettlogg spends his after school hours trolling Internet chat rooms and MySpace looking for the companionship of adolescent computer nerds. In this monologue he tells his psychiatrist how he avoids being caught.

PRINCIPAL PETTLOGG. There are certain words that aren't allowed, but you can get around'em. Example: "Sixty-nine" is vulgar, unless we're talking about the Vietnam war, a room number or a street address. "Come" is okay as long as it's not erotic. "I'm coming," strangely enough, is permissible, but "I cum when I see you in shorts" is not. "Suck" is fine as long as it's in reference to life or a sports team. Example: The Cubs Suck. The word "Oral" can only be associated with "Roberts" or "report." "Masturbation" is okay only when talking about art or an artist. You see AOL has on-line supervisors who listen in. Type a particular catchword and alarms. It's just like teaching, you gotta read the fine print. *(Beat.)* I'm a regular in fifteen different chat rooms and I've received warnings from all of them.

(Beat. PETTLOGG *becomes uncomfortable with what he is saying.)*

You don't record this do you? I record my morning announcement. Once I accidentally left it on and recorded my office technician talking about my salary. She didn't really say anything, but it got me thinking. You don't record this? I mean, not even privately for your own records? I know some psychiatrist record their sessions but you don't, right? Good. *(Beat.)* I found a smaller, little known chatroom that exercises no control whatsoever over content—True freedom of speech. So, well, it's like a magnet, perfect bait for little computer nerds…little boys with a desire to see the other side. But even there you gotta be careful. Not that I'm worried. As long as I watch what I say, which is not a problem, being in education. I'm good at self-editing. Watching every word.

(Beat. He leans back in his chair, loosens his tie and smiles.)

Doctor, would you mind if I took off my pants? It helped last time.

(He starts removing his pants.)

THE DEATH OF KING ARTHUR

Matthew Freeman

A devout and loyal Gawain stands before the stronghold of Joyous Gard, in the midst of a mighty siege, and demands that Lancelot answer for his crimes.

GAWAIN. The siege round Joyous Gard seems without end,
and daily struggles whittle down reserves.
The faces, one by one, fall by my side
and good men fall in legion by my side.
Our brothers, and our cousins, cut us down
and we, in turn, give them the peace of death.
If men beneath him will kill those they loved
Why can their coward cutthroat not respond in kind?
LANCELOT! Your doubtful nature tires
with every passing day, and stifles pity!
Where once I was distraught to wage upon
Your castle this unnatural, sibling siege…
Now I am hotter than the blood I spill!
Where once the sight pulled weeping woman drops
From eyes which looked only to peer on you,
Now their dry desire overtakes their fountains!
I'll cut until I cut your flesh at last!
You will release our good king's stolen wife
and cease dishonor on the Round Table!
You've taken every thing I made my life
and turned it inside out, till who can tell
what paradise was once? Camelot spits
and salts its soil with blood dripped spears in spite!
Your crimes surround you now, your faults compiled!
Soon I will judge thee as Jesus judges me
for each new soul I send to heaven's gates!

DEBT

Seth Kramer

Mosher, a gentle giant, reveals his long-held love to a sleeping Desha, explaining that he has been secretly painting her for years.

MOSHER. It's about… About how you're always there. Always with me.

(Pause.)

I've never been able to tell anybody this. Not Greg or Scott and especially not you. I mean, I used to think that this was wrong. You know, 'cause of you and Greg bein' together and all. I used to think…

(Pause.)

In my head.

(Pause.)

In my head you've always been with me. Like, when I'm watchin' a movie or drawin' or just sittin' by myself or somethin'. I can always put you there with me. Do it all the time. Hear things you'd say or see the things you'd do. When someone tells me a joke. I hear you laugh.

(Pause.)

I unlocked the studio this morning.

(Pause.)

I know you've always said you wanted to see more of my work… You'll be up in a few hours and—and I'll go out for a while. Leave you alone. I figure eventually you'll notice the door is open and go in. See all my paintings of you. And then…I don't know…

(Pause.)

I'm scared, Desha. Scared you'll…

(Pause.)

I look at you sometimes, when you're sleeping like this or when you're resting against me…and I want so bad to just reach out and…to…to slide my hand over yours, or run it along your arm or just feel your hair. I mean I want that so bad. And you tackle and hug me and you say things like— "I feel safe with you." When you make me aware of you. The two of us. Always sittin' together like we used to.

(Pause.)

I just wish…wish there was more, that's all. Wish I could…

(Pause, whisper.)

Do you know this?

(Pause.)

I never told you but I always thought—hoped that—somehow— you knew. That the little piece of you that I've been carryin' around in my head for all these years… That it somehow told you.

(Pause.)

It's the way you look at me sometimes…

(Pause.)

I unlocked the studio for you.

DEFACING PATRIOTIC PROPERTY

Tanya Barfield

A Man, alone. He wears a suit and tie. He is somewhat disheveled due to lack of sleep; he is somewhat hyper, too. At first, it may appear as if he is speaking to a psychiatrist.

MAN. You know, death, dying, decomposition, decay, *decidedly* not subjects I take lightly. I just want to tell you that. Let you know. Make that clear from the start. I mean, even this, even this act you and I are about to engage in is a relationship of sorts, right?

Doc, I was thinking…death, well, that's something that could benefit from a certain rehearsal process, even in the best of circumstances. Just as even the most lively conversation is only a replica of communication. But it's all a precursor to, well, you know, the big D. That little hang-nail, little nagging, little voice, little miniature rat scratching apart my thoughts: someday it's gonna happen. To you.

But for your part, it's not philosophical, right? You make a little cut, a tuck, an incision, vandalize eyes, ratify a new me.

(The doctor doesn't understand.)

You *are* a surgeon, aren't you?

(The MAN becomes a little miffed by the doctor's ineptitude. He becomes a little defensive but tries to explain things as clearly as possible.)

Look, I got the idea in South Dakota. Drove all the way to Beverly Hills. It took hours. Do you understand? Okay, maybe, I haven't been clear.

(Suddenly serious.)

I'd like to replace my face.

To look more…immortal. More stately. That's what you do, right? Anti-death, stave off time and uncertainty. But I'm a different case. I'd like to look more like the past.

(*The doctor clearly still doesn't understand. The* MAN *excitedly takes out a brochure.*)

I brought the brochure. Mount Rushmore National Memorial. Which one do you think would be more appropriate?

(*He looks at the brochure for a moment in awe.*)

They're so big. You can't tell from this picture, but they are. Bigger than big. Herculean heads. Colossal chins. Mammoth mouths. Granite grandeur. There I was dwarfed, beholden, to fantastic faces, the facade of founding fathers.

Teddy or Tommy, what do you think?… What? You don't?…

(*Disconcerted.*)

Well, what kind of plastic surgery do you do? Breast implants?! Oh, no, I don't think that's analogous at all.

You only deal with people that want to look younger?

All right, fine, fine, I'll find someone else. But let me ask you one thing, with such a narrow scope as yours, what is this nation coming to?

DIRTY LITTLE SECRETS

Jeffrey M. Jones

Frank is an aging, dying, world-famous singer with a "tough guy" image and hard-partying reputation, now trying to convince his fourth wife, Barbara, to release him from the hospital. His tone and demeanor hearken back to a time long past, when he was the swaggering leader of a pack of celebrities. In fact, his mind is wandering, and the ravages of his many diseases have left him child-like and petulant. The situation described in the monologue was originally reported in the tabloid press.

FRANK. Hey, hey, hey, baby—you know the score here.
Come on, what have I got, hunh? What've I got, Barbara?
I got what? I got a what? I got a heart failure, I got the liver failure,
I got the kidney failure,
Then I had the heart attack.
Then I had the stroke.
So now what? I got a cancer?
Come on, baby—you get the picture?
It's my time.
It's my time, Barbara.
And if I got a cancer, hell, so be it.
I'm dying, baby.
I'm dyin'…
And all I'm saying is I ain't gonna die in here in this joint on account of it stinks and I hate it, OK?
I just wanna go home…
Pour myself a drink
Light up a smoke…
Smoke a few last cigarettes.
Take a couple belts when the pain gets too bad.
And say the hell with it, baby.
Come on—what's God savin' me for, hunh?

What's He savin' me for:
I can't sing.
I can't eat.
I can't pee…
Can't make love to my beautiful wife.
What the hell is the point of it, baby? I want it over, I just want it over!
What the hell point is there living like this, there's no point at all. I want it over!
I just want it over, Barbara, I want it over and done with.
Why the hell don't somebody pull the goddamn, pull the plug, goddamn it! Just pull the plug, just pull the freakin' plug, and get me outta here!
You hear what I'm saying?

DOLLHOUSE

Theresa Rebeck

Neil Fitzpatrick has recently been released after spending eighteen months in jail for embezzlement. Fitzpatrick approaches Nora and threatens to blackmail her for the part she played in the embezzling if she doesn't convince her husband to give him a job.

FITZPATRICK. Yes he will! I should have figured it out yesterday when I, he was so—no way, if he knew? No way would be quite so cavalier, about whatever happens to me. *(Beat.)* I'm sorry. I have been trying, for months, to do this without dragging you into it, and I'm not getting anywhere. I'm a goddamned marked man and I'm not going down again without a fight. Now, I need help, and you are the one person who can help me, and you owe me. You and I did a dumb thing, together, and I covered for you, because I admit it, I admit it was my own damn fault I got caught. *(Beat.)* And your dad was good to me. I didn't want to, for his sake? But sentimentality only goes so far. I am trying—I want to see my kids. I want to be a father to them. And I don't want to get just stuck in this loop where prison is always hanging over your head, the only option you have is to break the law again because it's too hard not to. I want a decent life.

DRACULA

Mac Wellman

Jonathan, mind unraveling, speaks (partially in draculan) of the vampire's coming to England.

JONATHAN. But I escaped before he could do his wicked thing to me. Xxlld. Fpfptssc. So lovely there, we and the deadly.

I love Lucy. Kcm. Kcm. Bats. Bats. Interference from the future. Red dogs. Nuns. Goop. Magic lanterns. They warned me, they did. Can't say I wasn't warned. All in the diaries, all of it. He's going to England. Fresh blood. Needs it. Carfax. Large old stones. Easy terms. Qqqmc. Mina must learn to keep a proper diary. It's a horror. Like the movies. What's a movie? Moving world. Yes, desperation. Bonka bonka bonka bonk. And oh, the terrible twitching bag. The poor mother torn to pieces by hundreds of wolves in the awful courtyard.

Unspeakable. Xxxuuma. Fancy *him* at the British museum, as a sort of tourist! Looking at the Rosetta stone! Bat. Baseball bat. What in the name of heaven's that? Ah, the precious flask of slivovitz. I am a radio. What's a radio?

(Insane laughter.)

The milk that is spilt cries out not afterwards. A dog-eared diary, with real dog ears. I'd as soon eat molecules with chopsticks as dine with Count Deville. Dvlmnoa. Oao. Truly, the mad cause one to doubt the plan of God. Ha ha. He shall enter, yes, like those horrid bulls. Bonka bonk. Judge Moneybag will solve this. Beware the puppet show. The Black Dog shall land at Whitby by the North Sea. With his dirt. In big boxes. O. Then to downtown Whitby. Kkfffxxo. Get ye hammers and a spike. Oh, the diaries are so important! "What took it out?" What bloody well took it out indeed! Aye, there's the crux. O, a, u, O, a, u. X all the way to X' and half

---

the alcohol. X all the way to the walking fruit stand that is the Lord Mayor of Popinjay. X all the way to Kfx. Peppercorn in my pocket, and, oh, my mind's on fire. Flies, spiders, sparrows, cats. Peach Bottom reactor full of sleepers, o, a, u. He shall slide under the sash and stand before me, as the moon does in all her glory.

DRACULA

Mac Wellman

Dracula, appearing glorious in the night-sky, announces his mission, his essence, his purpose, in the grandest of terms.

DRACULA. I am pure *otherness*. The ridiculous little sham of human conceit does not involve me. I am pure absence, and am immune to the petty anxieties which trouble the shallow waters of humanity. I hear the music of other worlds, and understand the deadly elegance of absolute nullity. He who opposes me becomes the fruit of my ceremonial banquet. I burn no bones before the altar of strange gods. I waste no blood in obscene and futile rites of propitiation. I am clean. I am honest. I do not suffer the inexact furies of the moving world. My dream is vast, empty, stationary, most cunningly articulated, infinitely mutable and transmutable. It was me and my kind, the high lords of Ckm Ckm, who have opened one inch the door of perpetuity, and slipped beyond, leaving behind on the doorstep of your civilization only the pathetic corpse of a dead rat. Nothing, absolutely nothing. For I am pure otherness.

ELOISE & RAY

Stephanie Fleischmann

On the run from his relationship with his sweetheart, 16-year-old Eloise, Ray, 28 and an arthritic, has returned to Trouble, Texas, scene of the crime, where seven years go, he robbed a jewelry store with his best friend Jed, Eloise's brother, a caper that got him put in jail until recently. He thinks back on the missing Jed, who he hasn't seen for all this time.

RAY. I am one of the BOYS of the boys of the boys of the one of the—
Blood-brother-dynamic-duo-action-packed-//in-cahoots-smooth-moving-partners-in-crime—
Boys.
One of the— The two of us. Him. And me.
Like sand and water.

Because it's sand that gits in my joints. Sandpaper rubbing them down from the inside out. Rheumatoid. Old at 28. Because of him. Jed. His legs to my licketysplit thinker slippin' off and cementing my rheumy-eyed fate. Stiffin' me, stashing me away in the slammer, seven years, leaving me there for my bones to calcify. Who ever heard of a cowboy with arthritis?

Some might say it was me who stashed myself. Me. Who took the rap and let him walk away because his were the legs between us. What was I thinkin'? Momentary misstep, mammoth miscalculation. Seven years. Sandpaper pain scraping upside my head. Seven years. Adding up and taking over. So that all of a sudden it was time. To get even. To freeze him up. Wherever his legs had run their course. To throw a blow back in the direction of HIS stomach— When there she was. His. Even. Little sister twister shadow. So even. And me—I am—I was— One of the— She—is— She is a girl. Some strange kind of girl woman girl. All she gotta to do is look in my direction and the scraping pain is gone.

So I got even. I did what I had to do, only I didn't expect—I mean— How was I to know what I would feel? Too much girl-woman-girl for— For me. So I ditched her. What else could I do? I came back here. Me and Jed. Small town boys. Jewelry store hours from home. Nothing better to do than kick up some trouble. Here in Trouble, Texas, Scene of the Crime. Only— I been away from her one day and it's here. Sandpaper pain upside my head— Oh it's getting worse. It's bad.

What I need is water. My cureall. Eloise. Me and her. Like sand and water.

ELOISE & RAY

Stephanie Fleischmann

Ovid, Colorado. Ray, 28, is trying to make sense of his consternating relationship with his 16-year-old sweetheart, Eloise. This is his waking dreamscape.

RAY. What I like about Eloise is her size. She's a little bitty thing of a girl. Compact, so you can fold her up. Put her in a box and keep her. Fold her, hold her in your arms. That she is small means she is more easily mine. That she is small means I can pick her up off the ground. Light as a feather as she is, as a cloud as a shroud. I can lift her high up in the air. If that's what she needs. Hold her, fold her there for a while. Upside down. Hold her upside down and shake her. If she needs to be taught. Like the time I give her the pearl.

(He imagines ELOISE.)

RAY as ELOISE. What does it mean if I take it?

RAY. That you're mine.

RAY as ELOISE. And you? Are you mine?

RAY. I dunno Eloise, it's just a present.

RAY as ELOISE. But what'm I gonna do with it?

RAY. I dunno, Eloise. For chrissake. Eat it.

RAY as ELOISE. All right.

RAY. She swallows the pearl. So I don't got no choice. Cept to hold her, fold her. Upside down. And shake her. It's what she needs. I give her that pearl, see, because a pearl is sand and water. I am the sand and Eloise is the water. We got both of the two right here. Both of the two.

Ocean a million miles away.

That she is small means I can lift her high up in the air. Shake her long and hard, until the pearl comes spitting out. A pellet of a pearl. A pez. My Eloise a pez dispenser out of order, pez pellets round and hard and sharp as bbs made of steel coming flying out of her mouth. Little and small as she is, my BB gun of a girl. So I shake her and shake her and the pearl comes flying out and she is crying and that's when I hold her close, never once letting her feet touch the ground. Hold her, fold her there for a while. Because that's what she needs. She needs to be taught.

THE ELSINORE FOLLIES

Bill Warnock

The Gravedigger, after a romp with the Queen, admonishes the royal family about their excess lust and how it will inevitably lead to their downfall.

GRAVEDIGGER. It's becoming more obvious by the minute. Lust is the principal problem here in Elsinore.

The hanging prospect of being caught...*in flagrente*...with the Queen, may wonderfully concentrate the mind, but it threatens, mightily, to unman the body... *(He shrugs, pleased with himself.)*

Although, in the end, I performed well enough. I had no Royal complaint. *(Sly:)* It was, indeed, a consummation most devoutly to be wished. *(He breathes in and out, heavily, shakes his head, stunned by the experience.)* A remarkable woman!

But, mark my words, lust will bring them all down, here. Whatever it is that's going on, take a wager on it...it will be about lust. The problem with these royal parasites is boredom. They have nothing else to do. The odd skirmish on the ice against the Polacks...diplomatic posturings with neighbour States... But, apart from that, nothing. It's all heavy-handed revel, East and West; drunkenness...and lust. Right now, they're keeping one bleary eye on ambitious young Fortinbras passing through—so he claims—on his way to smite the Poles—him with one eye on the main territorial chance. The whisper goes that he's on Denmark's skirts to recover the lands lost by his late father. And this lot are so besotted with lust, that they believe him... *(Laughs:)* ...and give him license to cross flat, stale Denmark. There could be some profit in that...for a gravedigger.

Actor's Choice: Monologues for Men

FEEDING ON MULBERRY LEAVES

Lucinda McDermott

Winky, a convenience store owner, has had a minor stroke and begun painting his "visions." He talks to his wife about his fear of death.

WINKY. I been so worried about dying. About what would happen to the store. It's all I've ever done. If I died, would it die, too? Is that the sum total of my life, tax included? Got to where it was eating me up. I reckon that's why I had that Episode. After I painted my first vision, I had a glimpse of...a beyond.

(Refers to sign; "Are you dying to live or living to die?")

Like a window'd opened up. I made a bet with myself. Canceled my life insurance. I guess it was as if to say I'm dying to live! And let me tell you something Jean Grace Flint, once I did that, I had this feeling of life! For the first time in a long, long, time. I have new life! Okay. Okay. Maybe it wasn't too smart to cancel that policy. Last thing I wanted to do was for you to...please don't be mad at me. Please. I wanted to talk to you but you been so faraway, and I don't mean when you were at your sister's. Since you been back. Everything's different. Maybe it's me. Maybe I wasn't in my right mind. Maybe, maybe I'm not in my right mind. I don't know. I...feel, right jumbled. I'm scared. Bunny? I'm scared. I don't want to die. I don't want to die.

THE FIRST NIGHT OF CHANUKAH

Sheri Wilner

Morris is a spirit from the past who has returned to the site of his former home-stead in Devil's Lake, North Dakota to light the Chanukah candles. His farm is now an airport where he encounters David, a non-religious New York Jew, who is embarrassed by Morris's appearance and mocks the notion of there being such a thing as a "Jewish farmer," especially in North Dakota.

MORRIS. A scene must be made! I will not be forgotten! I will not allow my family be forgotten or to be made fun of by you. We were Jewish farmers. That is not a punch line of a joke, David. We did not work and suffer and mourn so that you could laugh at us.
We lived in *gebrenteh tsores*. In utter misery. My wife
Belka and our little girls Esther and Sarah. We came here not knowing where North Dakota was or anything about it.
Just that we would be free.
Our neighbor Velvel from Russia wrote and told us to come and so we came. When later I asked him, "Velvel, why didn't you tell us about the snow?" He said, "It's so horrible, I didn't know how to describe it."
He met us at the train station. For two days we traveled across the prairie and saw nothing but grass.
We had come from a city, the emptiness terrified us. My little Sarah asked, "Why has God taken everything away?"
At his house we were greeted by Velvel's wife, Ida and their twin sons. The boys had no shoes and wore rags on their feet.
Their home was made of mud.
One room they divided into two by a sheet.
One side was crowded with their beds.
The other side was the kitchen.
There were no chairs, they sat on sacks of flour.
Next to the stove was a pile of cow manure.

Actor's Choice: Monologues for Men

It was the only fuel they had.

Belka ran outside, the smell had made her sick. She became hysterical and refused to sleep near the filth.

But she had no choice.

We needed to live there while I built our own home. Velvel helped when he could, but the land was covered with rocks and he needed to clear them so the land could be plowed. I tried to work fast, but what did I know about building a house? Especially with mud, sod and dried grass? Winter came early, before the house was finished or the land was cleared. So we all lived together. Four adults, four children and sometimes the animals too. They would have frozen to death. Outside it could be forty degrees below zero. We needed to keep them alive for their eggs and milk. We kept the chickens under our beds.

The cow slept in the corner and *Oy gevalt*, you should never hear such snoring.

When I snored Belka pushed me onto my side and I stopped.

So one night she tried this with the cow and got a cloven hoof in the *pupik*.

We got used to the snoring.

We never got used to the cold.

We didn't have enough coal to last through the winter so we wouldn't burn any at night. In the morning we woke up and our clothes were frozen and icicles dripped on us from the ceiling. My babies' lips would be blue. Belka and I would be terrified. But we did not want our girls to see our fear and so we made a game out of it. "How many kisses will Papa give you today?" "How many will Mama?" And we would kiss their lips one, two hundred times until the color returned. For three winters that is how we lived.

(*Beat.*)

Do you have children?

FIVE FLIGHTS

Adam Bock

Tom, a professional hockey player and avid fan of ballet, describes the similarities between a hockey game and Russian ballet.

TOM. Of course. Oh yeah of course. I'll go and see it a couple of times. I love the ballet. Man I. I'm a hockey player you know so I love it, it's the same in a way, the movement, it's the same, I mean you take Russian nineteenth century ballet, it's just like a hockey game, it's got five acts, Russian ballet—five acts, act one, narrative it's the story told from beginning to end, act two's a vision, act three is mad scenes, act four the conclusion, act five, a little dance. Now hockey—the game is like the first act of the ballet when the story is told, it's the narrative, the hockey game itself. Then the second act, that's the moment of when it's over, in your mind's eye there's that moment, that critical goal, that incredible, amazing save, or the penalty, that something that was the defining moment that brought us here, it's like act two in the ballet, that moment is a vision. Act three, we won euphoria, or act three, we lost despair, madness, act four, the interviews, the commentary, the coaches' recap, it's all over it's all wrapped up this is what happened this and this and then act five I have to go dance because I'm so fired up I couldn't go to bed. I gotta go dance. I gotta keep moving. I love the ballet.

THE FIVE HYSTERICAL GIRLS THEOREM

Rinne Groff

Filipio, an Italian mathematician, has just learned that a high mathematical equation is imperfect. He confronts the frightening possibility that his mind is unable to grasp the infinite details of a man's life.

FILIPIO VERONESE. One hundred forty-seven quintillion, five hundred seventy-three quadrillion, nine hundred fifty-two trillion, five hundred eighty-nine billion, six hundred seventy-six million, four hundred twelve thousand, nine hundred twenty-seven is a very large number. A very terrifying number. How could one begin to plumb its depths? Our brains are forever evolving, but to such petty ends: shelter from the rain, knowledge of the berries, victory over the encroaching predators. Why could we not develop so as to see reality in a hundred dimensions, or to grasp an integer as vast as that? The number of water molecules in the Ocean? The number of miles in the Universe? The number of disappointments and crushing blows in the chronicle of Life, in the story of one man's life?

(FILIPIO *takes off his hat and lets it drop to the ground.*)

One hundred forty-seven quintillion, five hundred seventy-three quadrillion, nine hundred fifty-two trillion, five hundred eighty-nine billion, six hundred seventy-six million, four hundred twelve thousand, nine hundred twenty-seven water molecules in the Ocean? Imagine if I could know the meaning of that much water. Intimately. With Certainty. Imagine.

(FILIPIO *walks towards the water and in.*)

One hundred forty-seven quintillion, five hundred seventy-three quadrillion, nine hundred fifty-two trillion, five hundred eighty-nine billion, six hundred—

(He is gone.)

FREAK OF NATURE

Robert Alexander

Thomas Dumas, a brother from another planet, a man/alien born without a penis is telling his new bride Nava on their wedding night, about the planet he comes from. He is trying to seduce her with words as he prepares to make love to her telepathically.

DUMAS. Where I'm from, the air is red, the trees, grow upside down, under the ground. Dirt is blue, the ocean orange. The fish live in the ground, and birds don't have wings. They fly backwards, upside down, at the speed of light. Potatoes fall from the sky when it rains. And the people—we cry, only when we're happy, and we cry when we make love. And we make love with our minds, as we send out waves of pleasure and passion in quiet rays of fire and heat to the people we love. We copulate from the center of our brains. We can do it standing up in a crowded room, or laying down at the bottom of a pool. If you let me—if you can trust me, if you will allow me to turn your clock forward about a hundred thousand years, then you will experience an orgasm so intense, you will feel yourself levitate—your whole world will vibrate. Your toes will curl. Butter will come out of your pores. Your eyelids will flip back. The sun will burn through the trees as the light brightens your face and you will soak me inside of your syrup and you will drink me into your pores, and I will injaculate you with a pleasure so profound, we will both rise from the ground, as I drink up all your fears and catch all your tears. Inside our pleasure dome, I will mold you and hold you, as our love between the sheets, ends the war in the streets. Are you ready to come to that special place?

FREAKSHOW

Carson Kreitzer

The Human Salamander floats in a tank of water. Beyond his original webbed fingers and toes, he has willed himself to grow gills. He speaks to Amalia, the woman with no arms and no legs.

THE HUMAN SALAMANDER. Yes, no-one doubts your credentials. I am a mutation. That means change. Changed. And I have mutated. Into this half-human creature. Because just a bit of skin between the fingers and toes is fine for back home but it doesn't keep the crowd leaning in for a glimpse. So I became the Human Salamander. Until she saw me.

Staring eyes. Burning. The Human Salamander does not blush. The intricate network of veins and capillaries works differently than in ordinary humans. But there it was. I felt my skin growing hot. Under her gaze. How could she see me? Inside my guise? If it's happened once, it could happen again. That show could come when suddenly, an entire audience sees me. Some skinny kid, bloated with water. Sad. An entire audience suddenly overcome with revulsion and…pity. Now I know fear. She has ruined my life. A wandering pair of eyes, set the lie to the whole thing. She's cracked my tank. I won't notice the waterlevel sinking slow, just one day will come and I'll be naked. She doesn't even know what she's done. A day trip, idle staring. One moment of recognition—oh, that poor kid. He's about my age. Sitting there in a tank of water all day while people stare. Then moving on to see the other marvels. Then home. Cracked my tank and went about her life. Left me here to leak.

HAMLET: BLOOD IN THE BRAIN

Naomi Iizuka

H, grieving after his father's funeral, agonizes over the mourners' hypocrisy and his mother's cold adaptability.

H. i see him like i see you now, in the suit they put him in for the funeral at fullers, lyin there like he was asleep, like he was gonna open his eyes any second. people say that kinda shit, you know, but it's true. cause you don't, you don't see how they sew the mouth shut. you don't see how he's all cut up, how the insides are all, how they're all—fuck. and all the folks who was there, thousands of folks, people i ain't never even seen before, and all these females wailing and faintin and shit, strangers, you don't know them, you don't even know who the fuck they are, actin like they the ones, they the ones be grievin, and he ain't nothin to them, he ain't nothin to them. and the ones who should be grievin, his family, it's like they's all closed up. cold, cold to the bone. like they onto the next thing and they don't even have the time, they don't have the time. it's like for them, right, life jus fuckin closed over all that shit. ain't no hole, ain't no nothin. ain't no hurt. ain't no memory of hurt not even, like some poor motherfuckah shot in the back can't walk no more, but he remembers, he remembers the feeling in his legs, the tingle in his spine, ghost-like, he remembers the way it was. but it ain't even like that. it's seamless. you can't even see no scar.

HAMLET: BLOOD IN THE BRAIN

Naomi Iizuka

C runs down the rules of gangster survival.

C. all right then, first thing—are you listening? can you hear me? I said listen up!

don't be runnin your fuckin mouth. that's the first thing.

never never never get high off your own shit. don't do no stupid shit like that. think about it: how you make your paper? by getting fools sprung on dope. how does it work? cause the dope gets you sprung, stupid.

don't keep the shit you sell in the spot you stay.

and don't let no muthafucka do no dope in your crib. keep it all on the under: under crib, under car, switch your car to turn off the radar, keep it all on the under.

stash a grip to make bail quick, and don't be nickel and dimin when it comes to lawyers.

know some cats in the pen, jus in case.

but don't do no stupid shit, don't put yourself in harm's way. don't steal, don't speed, don't sleep on these youngsters.

and don't be no cowboy. ain't but one al pacino and scarface fuckin died in the end.

don't try to bust nobody in public, but don't be no punk. fire on a fool if need be.

and, remember: your pardners can't be reppin you if they sloppy. i don't care who the fuck they are. i don't care if they're blood. i don't care if they're your cousin, your brother, your brother's son, i don't care who they are. cut they ass from the team if they get loose or sloppy. do what you need to do, not what you want to do. handle your business.

HAMLET: BLOOD IN THE BRAIN

Naomi Iizuka

H, in an inexorable path of revenge, fantasizes about escaping with O.

H. i guess i'm thinkin how it is that i actually get to talk to you for real.
i'm thinkin how nice it feels to hear your voice up close.
how shiny your lips are.
it's like your lips are shining.
it's like you're shining.
i ain't never seen no shine or sparkle like that.

i'm thinkin what'd happen if we got in my impala and just kept driving.

if we just left here and went somewhere else, someplace faraway, new york city atlanta georgia miami beach florida, white sand and blue blue ocean, a whole different ocean.

do you ever wonder what it'd be like if we was born someone else, different mother, different father, different blood running through your veins?

you ever wonder how we could leave the past in the past? be somebody else? walk a different road? cause see, i know how this story goes, the only way it can go, everyone knows how this story goes, live by the sword, die by the sword, everybody knows, that's how it goes, the oldest story under the sun.

do you ever wonder how it feels to be on the outside looking in?

do you ever wonder how it feels to be in a jam so thick you can't find a way to slide through, like being on the inside, like being locked up in a fuckin cage, like everywhere you turn is a dead end, is a brick wall, and there ain't no key, there ain't no way out.

HAND JIVE

Lew Holton

Taylor Armstrong, a struggling writer who has lived in the shadow of his recently deceased father's (Andy) literary fame, speculates to his wife about what might have festered beneath some of his father's secret self-destructive ways.

TAYLOR. Once, when I was a kid—twelve, thirteen, somewhere around there—I was checkin' out the closets. It was around Christmas; I was snoopin'. And I found this box of stuff. Old stuff from the war—medals, papers, stuff like that. ...You know, he never told me exactly what happened to his arm. He just said an airplane blew up and he got hurt. Never sat down and told me the whole story. And once I found out, I never told him I knew. ...In the box, there were these ribbons and pins, and two separate boxes—like jewelry boxes. One box had his Purple Heart; the other held a Navy Cross. I didn't know then what a big deal that was. Later, one summer when I was home from college, I looked around and found that box again. That time I looked through the papers and found the citation that went with the Cross. That's how I found out what happened.

It was the last few months of the war. He was aboard a destroyer in the Sea of Japan. They were attacked by Japanese planes. He shot down this...no. No, he didn't just "shoot down" a plane—he SAVED an entire ship. *(Short laugh.)* An entire ship! Right now, there's this humongous gray Navy ship floating around out there someplace 'cause my Dad saved it. *(Short pause.)* I hope that's not one of those "after-life" questions...like from St. Peter or somebody... *(In St. Peter's voice, whatever that sounds like:)* "What did you save, Andy?" *(Snapping to attention, saluting with his left hand, and answering as ANDY:)* "One United States Navy destroyer and countless American sailors, sir!" *(As St. Peter again:)* "Excellent! And you, Taylor?" *(As himself:)* Ummm...some old baseball cards? *(Short*

---

pause.) I mean, it's weird, ya' know? You think you've got your old man pegged, and suddenly you're reading stuff like "ran through the twisted, burning metal," and "above and beyond the call...". All this John Wayne shit. ...Anyway—even though he saved the ship, I guess some of his friends didn't make it. You've heard of survivor guilt? I'm not sure it didn't just take all those years for that guilt to work its way to the surface...like a piece of old shrapnel.

HATE MAIL

Bill Corbett and Kira Obolensky

Preston is a neurotic Midwesterner whose letter exchanges with Dahlia began with a complaint letter. Dahlia has just discovered that Preston is the "Mysterious Gentleman" who bought all twelve of the photographs at her art show— her nude photographs. Preston writes a letter in return, and encloses a gift.

PRESTON.

Dear Dahlia:

Ah, splendid detective work! Yes, I was that mysterious gentleman caller. (Told you I was coming to Gotham…and I'm very serious about my travel!)

Your photographs now adorn the south wall of my new condo in swingin' Downtown Minneapolis, a 12th-story bachelor pad worthy of Hugh Hefner. I like to move every six months or so—it's become sort of a hobby.

But I digress: good to hear from you again! And I'm sorry to hear that the crrrrrriiiitttiiiics piled up on you. You shouldn't get upset about it, you know. This stuff is completely arbitrary. They could have canonized you just as randomly; the coin simply landed on the other side.

I for one stand by your tremendous talent—even if I am, apparently, very much alone in this. Your instinct for composition—the way you employ light!—remain a source of inspiration to me. When the photos were delivered here, I spent the next three days arranging and re-arranging them in my new den.

But why are you so upset that I have these? After being hung at a public gallery in Manhattan for weeks, where every Tom, Dick and Enrique could ogle them! I assure you I don't sit in the middle of

---

the room all day, staring at them, masturbating. I have a fine assortment of other materials for that purpose.

Why did I buy them? You touch me. Your face is so sweet, so delicate and vulnerable; but your gaze is so assured. Your ideas leap out of the picture—your struggle looks so noble, your passion is so real, and I'm aware that mine is not. And admittedly, yes, your nude body isn't hard to look at, either.

But to make you feel better, let me offer, as the philosopher Hannibal Lechter would say, "quid pro quo."

Enclosed are not twelve but thirteen photographs of me, as naked as a human can be, full frontal self-portraits done with a timer by the shores of White Bear Lake. Yes, a baker's dozen of my bare booty, in a variety of dignified poses. In comparison with yours, of course, my camera work is rank amateur—complete with the glowing demon-red eyes. But it's not the eyes that matter most here, is it?

Two disclaimers:

1) I am usually a tad trimmer. I've gained 23 pounds since going on the meds. And yet I let myself be displayed, revealed, consumed by you. I think that's pretty goddammed brave, don't you?

2) It was a very cold day out.

Your Soulmate in Search of a Kodak Moment, Preston.

HAZARD COUNTY

Allison Moore

Tim, 40s, white, Midwestern. Middle-class, dressed in business casual. His coworkers might be surprised to learn that he's a fan of "The Dukes of Hazard."

TIM. It's escapism, pure and simple. Don't get me wrong. There's a time and place for serious discussions, but after a long day, I'll take a couple of car chases and the sight of Catherine Bach poured into those itty-bitty shorts anytime. I mean, sure, it's formulaic. You know the bad guys are always going to get caught, the Dukes are going to be exonerated of whatever ridiculous charge Roscoe's trumped up. And Cooter will always be able to fix the General. But there's also. Well, now I'm going to get philosophical, but. You know, there's an ethic to the show. If you really watch it. Basic stuff. Family comes first. Respect your elders. If something breaks, you fix it. If someone needs help, you help them. It's not all that far off from Little House on the Prairie, you know? It's really not. But you don't see Laura Ingalls still in prime time syndication now, do you? No sir. She's on in the middle of the day. But twenty years later, The Dukes of Hazzard are still there. And you know why? Because underneath everything that happens, there is always an acknowledgement that the law is never on the common man's side. The law is there to protect the Boss Hoggs of the world, keep the fat man fat and the common man down. Maybe they are just a couple of rednecks with a hot car. But at least they know the score and they aren't afraid to say it. Any day now, I'm gonna be staring at a pink slip, trying to figure out how to pay for my COBRA insurance, while my boss' boss reports to the shareholders that through "aggressive cost-cutting measures" they're all gonna be a million dollars richer then they were last quarter. It's nice to turn on the TV and see someone out there fighting the system like two modern day Robin Hoods. So sue me if for one hour each week I want a little piece of that.

HAZARD COUNTY

Allison Moore

Blake, a spoiled but earnest young TV producer, has come to a small Kentucky town in search of a story that will turn his career around. He gains the trust of a local woman, Ruth, and now has to confess that he isn't actually a news producer—yet.

BLAKE. I'm a reality TV producer. That's what I've been doing for the past, ten years. And it's stupid. It is! It's asinine, there's nothing honest about it. But it doesn't matter now. Because I'm telling you, this is the beginning, Ruth. I am finally going to get to work as a journalist! There is no way that Jack can turn this story down. Never again will I have to provoke people into, barking, or— That's what reality TV is! I mean, I don't think that it's responsible for the demise of our entire culture, but, there is a stigma in the industry. And once people hear this one thing—one thing— about you, and forget it, they've judged you. It's not just that, it's. Everyone always asks how we find so many people willing to be filmed in such humiliating ways. But once the camera is on, you have no control over how you are presented. We are not obligated to the truth. We are there to construct entertainment. Take things out of context, or splice it together with, with anything. God, there was this barber in Fresno—this was for a late night cable slot. He was this ancient man with a huge mole on the side of his face. And we interviewed him about his trade—very benign, what sort of clippers he used, and did he do shaves and what about beard trimming. He was the most patient man, which, in TV terms, is boring. So I started fucking with him, you know, playing dumb, repeating the same questions over and over, until he got frustrated and started shouting, "That's what I said! Men like a clean shave! It's got to be smooth!" And I edited the whole thing with footage of a bunch of strippers getting bikini waxes.

Shot of him shouting, "It's got to be smooth!"

Sound of a stripper moaning.

Close up on his mole.

Shot of the stripper saying "Men like it smooth."

Shot of him, "Well, yes I like it smooth, and so does my wife."

Shot of his wife raising her eyebrows.

Shot of the stripper spreading her legs.

It's stupid, and low brow, but that's how it's done. And as long as you get consent...?

But I am not going to do that anymore. My father's best friend is Congressman Ripley, California. I got him to agree to name me to the Committee, and then I pitched the whole thing to Fox News. Jack gave me a car and a camera and thirty days to come up with feature stories they might want. If I do, they'll hire me. Couple of days. I am an unemployed producer who had to beg someone to let me work for free. That's the truth. I know it sounds pathetic, but I am not going to be ashamed anymore, Ruth. I did it. After three years of trying to get anyone to give me a break, I took matters into my own hands.

HAZARD COUNTY

Allison Moore

Jeffery, 30s, white, originally from South Carolina, but now living in a big city. Educated, witty and fashionable. Gay, but not flamboyantly so. A very direct manner.

JEFFERY. Imagine:

You're driving on the back roads of Georgia. You're alone. It's getting on dusk. The roads are crap. And your car breaks down. You're stuck. And two young men, in an old car, happen along. And they stop—so they say—to help you. You're in luck. They say their friend Cooter can fix your car. Well, they'd be happy to give you a ride up to the roadhouse. It's just up the way a piece. It's a little dive with no windows and one door, where lots of other men just like them will be consuming large amounts of alcohol. There's a phone there, they can call for a tow, if you'll just, hop in back…?

Are you imagining it?

Oh, I know.

(He hums the first few bars of "Dueling Banjos.")

Of course I watched it. I watched it avidly, as a child. And I'll tell you, part of me wanted to be in it. And I don't mean in a child-star kind of way, I mean part of me wanted to live inside the show. I wanted to drive around in a fast car with these strong, capable, incredibly sexy men who would do anything for each other. All right, every third episode, one or the other of them had a love interest. But everybody knew Bo and Luke had a bond that no trashy Boar's Nest whore could break. And being cousins never stopped anybody in the South, right? But note that I say only part of me wanted to live in this world. Because interesting thing is? Even as a fourth-grader, I knew that if Hazzard were a real place, and Bo and

Luke were real people? They would not befriend me. Oh no. They'd have kicked my ass if I met them. And somehow I knew this, watching the show in my parents' living room in Charleston, South Carolina at the age of nine.

I was telling a friend here in Providence about all this, and he said to me, "What does this say about you, Jeffery? That as a child you were attracted to these men whom you believed would harm you?" And I said, that's not the question. The question is: Where did I learn to be afraid of Southern men? I know when, approximately. By the age of nine, at least. But where, how, had I learned to believe that no matter how kind, and altruistic, and handsome he seemed? Well, if he has a certain accent, and especially if he's poor, he is capable of violence at any moment.

And what do you do, how do you live, if that man who everybody assumes those things about, is you?

IPHIGENIA IN TAURIS

translated by Edward Seymour
from the play by Johann Wolfgang von Goethe

Orestes, a warrior in his early twenties who is affected by bipolar disorder, has collapsed unconscious on recognizing Iphigenia as his sister and admitting to their mother's murder. Here he recovers consciousness, but experiences a hallucinatory vision—indicated in the text by the change from iambic to dactylic metre—of reconciliation between his warring ancestors.

ORESTES. *(Awaking from a stupor and sitting up:)*
Another one! Give me one last cool chalice
Of Lethe's waters to revive my senses.
Soon the convulsive force of life will spill
Out of my bosom; soon my calmer spirit,
Surrendering to the fountain of oblivion,
Will join you shadows in eternal mist.
Be kind to me, and let me be refreshed
By your calm presence from all harassment!
—What is that whispering among the trees,
What are those rustling noises in the darkness?
—They're coming now, to see the guest arrive.
Who are these people in their splendid robes,
Convivial as a prince's wedding party?
They walk in peace, both young and old, both men
And women; godlike in manner and appearance,
These drifting figures. —Ah, I know, they are
My ancestors, my house! —For with Thyestes
Atreus comes, in confidential murmurs;
The boys dart mischievously to and fro.
Is there no enmity between you now?
Has vengeance been extinguished with the sunlight?
Then I too must be welcome, and permitted

To join your ceremonious procession.
Welcome, ancestors! Orestes greets you
As your descendant, the very last man;
What you have sown, he has now reaped:
Laden with evil, he has come down;
But here all heavy burdens are eased:
Take him, O take him into your company!
—Atreus, greetings—and you, Thyestes.
Here we are all released from our enmity.
—Show me my father, whom I've seen only
Once in my life. —Is that you, Father?
Walking so trustingly at Mother's side?
If Clytemnestra can give you her arm,
Orestes can go up to her now
And speak to her, say: This is your son!
Both of you, look! Give him your welcome.
Back on the earth, in our own house
Murder was certainly the only greeting,
And ancient Tantalus's generation
Finds pleasure on the far side of night.
You say I'm welcome! You'll let me in?
O take me to see him, see the old man!
Where is my ancestor? Let me behold him,
Much-loved old father, greatly respected,
Who once advised even the Gods.
Why do you hesitate, turning away?
Why? Do those close to the Gods also suffer?
Alas! The almighty have fastened in strong
Fetters of bronze to the shoulders of heroes
Horrible torments, for ever and ever.

KING O' THE MOON

Tom Dudzick

It is a night in July, 1969, just hours before Neil Armstrong makes his historic first step on the moon. Eddie Pazinski, 25, about to be shipped out to Vietnam, is speaking to his younger brother, a seminarian.

EDDIE. Yeah, so Iggy gets up, flicks off the TV, walks out of the house. Walked right past me, didn't even see me. Found him sittin' on a garbage can in the alley. Says he wanted to smash the TV. Says, "Ooh, wow, Armstrong's gonna walk on the moon, be a hero. Think he's ever <u>heard</u> of Vietnam? Let him walk where I was for a day. The moon got booby traps every ten feet? They got leeches on the moon? Does he sleep in a moon swamp every night? Wake up, face covered with mosquitoes?" Huh? He told me about the people over there. They don't want him there. He's there to free them, they booby trap his bus and blow it up. The shooting. When it starts nobody knows where it's coming from, or who's doing it, or who to shoot at, or when to stop. Says we got kids over there handling explosives. A hand grenade went off during chow— one dead, twenty wounded. And he says there's no "cause" over there that anybody cares about. Just hate your enemy, kill, survive and come home. No, don't start with that "God will be with me" crap! I'll kill you if you do! He says God's not over there! There's just one thing I want from you. I want you to make sure Maureen marries somebody decent. Not right away. I mean, after a while. Don't laugh at me, shut up and listen! No bums. You know what I mean? Gotta have a decent job. Gotta be Catholic. And nobody from around here. Maybe from where I used to work. Doesn't have to be rich, but somebody, I dunno, artistic. She likes to talk about drawin' and dancin' and stuff. And he's gotta like kids. Check him out.

LANGUAGE OF ANGELS

Naomi Iizuka

Seth, whose girlfriend Celie vanished in a cave, imagines searching through complete blackness.

SETH. There are parts of this country out this way, pure and wild, unknown to man, no human eyes have ever seen, cave country it is, hundreds of miles of caves, stretching and twisting underground, passages and tunnels and wide open chambers, pools so deep you'd never touch the bottom—

Down in the caves, you gotta know what you're doing, gotta know what you're up against, you gotta remember, keep it in the back of your mind always, and if you do, if you know your way around, you can get from here to there and back again. Some of these boys, they know the caves pretty well, some of the caves down there, you can even see traces, paper, candles, broken glass, see the names spray painted on the wall. Party down there in one of those caves, take your girl, a case of beer, whatever, get high.

I did that once. Used to. This was, this was before.

People from these parts, everybody knows the stories, somebody gets lost down in the caves, some guy, high or drunk, wanders deeper and deeper, passes out, wakes up in that pitch black darkness, can't remember how he came to be there, where exactly he is, which way he needs to go to get out, and it's so black, it's like you can't even see your hand when it's this close to your face, dark, you can't imagine how dark it gets, and now he's getting spooked, and turned around, he can't remember how he got to where he is, which way is in and which way is out, and he starts walking faster and faster, twisting and doubling back, making a wrong turn somewhere along the line, going the wrong way, deeper and deeper into the blackness so black, nothing else like it, nothing feeling right, the way the tunnel turns, and all he knows is his heart beating, and the feel of the stone underfoot, the feel of the stone wall damp and rough against his palm, sound of water dripping, and somewhere far away, the rustling of a thousand wings, all the things you become aware of in that darkness, tiny things, and how they all feel wrong this time around, and in your heart you know, you know this isn't the way, this isn't right, and slowly you feel the panic come on, and slowly you understand just how lost you are, and what that means, and you lose all sense of which way is back and which way is forward, all sense of time, and all you feel now is your lungs and your sweat, cold sweat, and the space so narrow now like a grave, until you got no room to stand, on your hands and knees, crawling in the blackness, trying to see, trying to get back, when all of a sudden you see it—

Something up ahead—

A light, a shaft of light— Flickering, faint, a light—And now you see it glimmering, glowing, a steady glowing— There is a light— And you crawl faster and faster towards that light, towards that brightness just up ahead, just at the end of the tunnel, if you just go a little further, just a little further, you're almost there, almost, so close you can almost touch it with your hand, and then bang— You hit a wall of stone, and the light vanishes like it was never there.

What it was, what it is.

When it gets that black, in the deepest part, in the blackest part, the eyes play tricks. The mind plays tricks.

Celie? Celie girl, is that you—?

LAPIS BLUE BLOOD RED

Cathy Caplan

Rome, 1612. Orazio has just been informed that his sixteen year old daughter was raped by the man he trusted to teach her how to paint. Orazio berates his orderly and tenant for their irresponsibility in the care of his daughter, holding them largely accountability for the rape. In turn, he promises to destroy the teacher's life and force him out of Rome.

ORAZIO. No, we won't eat. *(In Tuzia's voice:)* Why doesn't everyone sit down? *(In his own voice:)* Or why doesn't everyone line up against the wall. And I can hit you one after the other. No. I'm not going to eat your food. I'm going to eat you. How do you like that? I am running three miles each way back and forth twelve times a day between this house and up that mountain—hill—chaos— making sure you have fresh pigment, making sure you have work, making sure you have some one to model for you, making sure the twelve idiots who work for me keep painting even when I am out of the room for one second. Everyone says your problem Orazio is you're taking on too many jobs, taking care of too many people, too much meat on the fire. But I say, oh I have my safety net. If I fall off the scaffolding, that's bad. But, if I fall off a scaffold and I've got someone to catch me, or a rope to catch on to, I'm doing all right. If I have an upstairs tenant who happens to be a pretty close friend of mine, who happens to not pay a ducat in rent, who assures me, that while I am at work, I can leave the worries of my household behind me, that she will watch my daughter like a hawk, take care of my baby boy like a mother, that is my rope. That is my safety net. I'll worry about your daughter. I am forty-five years old. You are thirty-three years old and you are fucking my daughter who is sixteen years old. Under my roof, in my studio. And what chance do I have of marrying her off now. That makes me mad. Very mad. I'll destroy you. You will never get near this house again.

You will never get into the academy. You will never work in Rome. You will never touch her again. I promise you that. Let me build a cross and I'll nail all three of you to it. And when you're finished you can hang me on it too. And then you can come to my funeral ten minutes later. And you will not get one more shred of her and not one more shred of this either.

(ORAZIO *picks up the money.*)

Not one more shred of her.

LAST LOVE

Peter Papadopoulos

Outside Charles and Lucida's house an international terror war looms, and surveillance helicopters hover continuously overhead. Inside the house two couples are also at war. Lucida is sleeping with Jim, her husband Charles' best friend. Charles has moved his new girlfriend, Sally (Jim's ex-fiancé) into the guest bedroom. A drunken poetry slam ends with Sally railing against ex-lover Jim and storming off. Charles surveys the wreckage and struggles to make sense of the violence raging inside and outside his house.

CHARLES.
This is the kind of violence that starts wars.

The solemn and thoughtless rejection
by one's intimate partner
can force a man to take refuge
to find a place of solace
so they start wars
seek out slights to retaliate against
find potential threats that need crushing
you have weapons of mass destruction
No we don't—yes you do—no we don't—yes you do—no we
don't
BATTABOOM BATTABOOM BATTABOOM
because wars are comfortable
for those who cannot be comforted.

And I know it's hard to remember a time
before the world was always at war
before every low-flying plane was a missile
before every backpack was a bomb
before every brown man was a foreigner
before every out-of-town license plate was memorized

but for some men
it is safer to be at war
all-out war
with bullets whizzing by
and grenades going off next to you
and maybe you lose a limb
and your dreams of being a guitarist
or maybe you lose your best friend
or even your own life
but to be at war
can still feel safer
than to be at peace
in such a violent way.

THE LEGEND OF SLEEPY HOLLOW

adapted by Christopher Cartmill
from the story by Washington Irving

Ichabod Crane is the superstitious and ambitious schoolmaster in the village of Sleepy Hollow. He has fallen in love with one of his pupils, the daughter of a wealthy local farmer, Katrina Van Tassel. On his way to meet his beloved, he happily celebrates the beauty and abundance of the surrounding autumnal countryside.

ICHABOD. Happy I am! Certain it is. The sky is clear and serene, and nature wears that rich and golden livery which we always associate with the idea of abundance. The forests have put on their sober brown and yellow, while some trees have been nipped by frosts into brilliant dyes of orange, purple, and scarlet. Streaming files of wild ducks high in the air; the bark of the squirrel from the groves of beech and hickory nuts, and the pensive whistle of the quail at intervals from the neighboring stubble field. Small birds taking their farewell banquets. In the fullness of their revelry, they flutter, chirping and frolicking, from bush to bush, and tree to tree, capricious from the very profusion and variety around them. Oh, the treasures of jolly autumn! Vast stores of apples, some hanging in oppressive opulence on the trees, some gathered into baskets and barrels for the market, others heaped up in rich piles for the cider press. Great fields of Indian corn, with their golden ears peeping from their leafy coverts, and holding out the promise of cakes and hasty puddings! And the yellow pumpkins lying beneath them, turning up their fair round bellies to the sun! Giving ample prospects of the most luxurious pies! The fragrant buckwheat fields. The odor of the beehive. And, oh, imagine those dainty slap jacks, well-buttered, and garnished with that honey by the delicate little dimpled hand of Katrina Van Tassel!

LOBSTER ALICE

Kira Obolensky

The great Surrealist Salvador Dali is in Hollywood, working on a short ani-mated film at a big studio that has just started turning "Alice in Wonderland" into a cartoon. After several Surrealist delay tactics, Dali tells his studio co-horts the story of his short animation, called "Destino."

DALI. I will tell you Dali's story.

> *(What follows is the stage version of an animated surrealist ballet, in which* DALI *acts out all the parts.)*

It is a myth. It is a tragedy. It is a love story. As every story should be.

We begin at the edge of the world. Luminescent, phosphorescent, fluorescent, tumescent! The edge of the world looks like the cliffs of Dover. A watch running out of time. A drain sucking a sinkful of water.

The edge of the world. Stand on it and you will find yourself near the edge of death. Or life.

A young girl about to be an old woman. We are, each of us, the culmination of every instant, every part of our life, from the past to the future.

And, I might add, it's a moment I personally adore. When beauty flares for one brief fling before settling into something ordinary. My heroine.

We first see her in a field, picking strange daisies as big as trees. She is oblivious to the eyes that gaze upon her. Eyes as large as the world. Eyes in the daisies. Eyes in her own eyes.

Chronos, the god of Time. Time looks like a blank watch, a portrait of a dead person, ice, a beautiful boy. He will be her lover.

What would you do if you stared Time in the eyes? What will she do when she stares into his eyes, which are like pearls and chocolate.

She sees him first in the flowers, and then in the sky. And perhaps someplace more ordinary. A swimming pool.

First there is an introduction.
And then there is a seduction.
Seduction is a red cape.
You Tempt Me.
Seduction is a crevasse, wet with sweat.
Seduction is easy when Chronos is in the bed.

The second movement is very seductive. I see a plethora of creatures, each more fantastic than the last. I want floozies and flotsam, daggers spitting out of the mouth of a tiger. Nipples like mountains, climbed by a kiss. A woman sodomized by her own chastity.

A puddle of lust. A puddle of pride. A puddle from Paris. A puddle of puddles, each filled with desire.

The heroine of my story, I'd call her Alice only that would upset you. The heroine of my story and Chronos unite.

They make monsters together.

The monster of shame. Shame is a woman with a mustache and a cake on her head.

The monster of lust, a wet seal.

The monster of youth, which looks like a watch. Water rushing down a drain. A beautiful boy.

The lust, shame and youth leak into the world, in a chaos of umbrellas shaking themselves of excrement.

And there is rain.

The sound of ripping paper.

You Tempt Me
And You Tempt Me.
And You Tempt Me.

There is blood. Perhaps.
There are tears
Which wash the earth clean.
And dissolve the story.

Leaving traces on the screen and in the memory. Of all that we search for. All that we love.

The sad sounds of violins.

      (A beat. DALI *spent, throws himself again on the couch.)*

Magnificent. That was magnificent.

LOVE

Stephen Belber

Rick, after finding his head waiter and busboy hanging out in the restaurant's basement, expounds upon the difficulties of managing the dinner rush with an incompetent staff.

RICK. What the hell are you two doing down here!? I been lookin' all over for you! What am I, an asshole?—what am I, an asshole with cream cheese with chives?! I got fifteen tables seated up there, I got parties of eight ordering goddam individual salads, I got deuces wanting Chianti, I got a family of six ordering french fries with goddam milk-cream gravy, that's right, milk-cream, *milk-*cream, I said *milk-cream*!!! And now I got *you* two hanging out down here jackin' each other off! Huh? What're you doin'?—*(Gesticulating.)*—a little jerky dance? huh?—you jerkin' each other?! you smokin' dope? what is it? Huh, Bill?—smooth guy, you got an answer for me? You're my best goddam waiter, you're the only one who's done a taste test on the Dubeouf Beaujolais and you're down here in the basement freakin' out on me! What is it with you?! And *you*, Tommy Kid, pipsqueak, what the hell is this?!— *(RICK pulls a fork from the breast pocket of his shirt.)* You're supposed to *check* the goddam fork prongs before you put 'em in the silver trays! You see this?! what is this?—I'll tell you what this is, it's a goddam piece of hamburger fat from the house meatloaf is what it is!! You're a fucking busboy, kid, you're *this* close from being fired when you're doing the job *perfectly*! You keep screwin' up like this and you'll be out on the welfare line with all them crack mothers before you can say 'Bob's your fuckin' uncle'!!! Now listen, I got ketchup bottles that need reconsolidation, I got bus tubs that need to go to the dish room, candles need to get on the tables by six, I got a goddam floor up there needs more sweepin' than a goddam minefield, an' I got *you* sittin' down here lookin' like you wanna blow the goddam head waiter!! *(Beat.)* What's the deal with the twine, Bill?

THE LYNCHING OF LEO FRANK

Robert Myers

Alonzo Mann, age 84, has come forward to testify before the Georgia Pardons and Parole Board to exonerate his former boss, a Jewish factory manager, Leo Frank. Mann recalls the day 70 years earlier when Frank was lynched by a gang for a child murder, a crime Mann is certain Frank did not commit.

ALONZO. I'm on my way to work when I hear the news. No one actually tells me. Word just spreads, like a fire burning out of control. I want to run fast as I can back home, ask my mama if it's me who's responsible for him that's hanging from that tree in Marietta, but I don't run. I just stand there in the middle of Forsyth Street, with streetcars and automobiles coming at me, drivers cursing, horses rearing up in confusion, horns honking like they're way off in the distance, but the only sensation I feel is the quaking in my own chest. All of a sudden, I see his face in front of me, staring with them big bug eyes. He looks just like he did that Saturday morning, his skin milky white, that long pointy nose holding up his spectacles. He looks so real, I close my eyes, but when I do I see something much worse. Him, hanging from that oak tree, his hands cuffed in front of him, a kerchief covering his face, a burlap sack instead of proper trousers wrapped around his legs, and a group of men in overalls standing below him with their arms crossed in front of them like they're looking at a religious object.

(Beat.)

Most of them want to burn the body on the spot, but some judge steps in, says he doesn't disagree with what's been done, but reminds them Mr. Frank's got a family too that at least deserves the body. But when they cut him down, one man gets so angry he stomps Mr. Frank's face until there's nothing left of that long pointy nose. And then they tear his clothes to bits and cut up little pieces of the rope and take pictures of themselves with the body for souvenirs until the judge arrives with two nigrahs who carry him off in a wheelbarrow. That afternoon, hundreds of them shove their way into Greenberg's Funeral Home to get a glimpse of the body. The next morning, Mrs. Frank puts his casket on the train and takes him back up to Brooklyn to bury him and puts a headstone on his grave that says, "Nothing Changes." I reckon he's resting a mite better up there.

...KS NEEDS WOMEN, BUT NOT AS MUCH AS ARNOLD SCHECTER

Rich Orloff

J.D., a guy who views himself as quite the ladies' man (a view probably not shared by any woman who has met him), tries to empathize with his friend Arnold's romantic woes by sharing his own recent frustrations with women.

J.D. Women, they're so surface. They say *we're* surface, but they're the ones who are surface. We may fantasize about making love to tantalizing women whose firm, delicious bodies make our glands charge into overdrive, but when push comes to shove, we'll screw anyone. We don't have the arrogance women have.

Last night, I went out with this chick. Now it's not like it's the first date or nothing that I'm putting the moves on her. It's already the second date; third, if you count the time I drove her to her foot doctor.

So I take her out to a fancy restaurant, you know, with tablecloths, and when we're done eating, and I let her finish, I pick up the tab, leave a nice tip, 11.6%, and then we go to a first-run movie, and I buy this expensive tub of popcorn, and I don't even care how much she's having—roughly two-fifths, and then after the movie we go out and I buy her a couple of drinks, the fancy kind, with those cherries that give you cancer, and then I take her back to her place, and I tell her she's beautiful, beautiful, *beautiful*, and then she says, get this, she says she's still not ready to have sex with me. And I'm so stunned, I just blurt out, "What do women want?" And she says, "I like my popcorn *buttered.*"

MEN SUCK

J. Holtham

A man. A woman. A bar. It's closing time and the battle of the sexes is about to take a revolutionary turn...

JOHN. Men suck. It's true. We do. We do. Some guys are afraid to say it. But we all know it's true. We do. We do. I mean, it's like all the time, you know. You, a woman, an attractive woman, want to go out. Have a nice time. Have a drink. You think, "How many nights have I sat in this stupid apartment, choking down this take-out dinner, watching this same show that I never found funny? Too many. Tonight, I'm gonna go out. I'm gonna put on a nice shirt and clean jeans and go to a bar and buy myself my favorite drink." A seabreeze, right? Who doesn't love a seabreeze? You go out. You sit there and drink your drink and think your thoughts. And what happens. Some guy who thinks playing high school football made him God comes over to you, smelling of cheap beer and cigars and wants to take you home with him. Thinks that you're melting in the presence of the hot-blooded American MALE. But they never notice the plastic smile, the forced laughter, do they? Them. Huh. There I go, trying to separate myself from them. But I am one. A man. Accident of birth. Smoke?

(MAGGIE takes out her own cigarette. JOHN lights it for her.)

And let's say you get one. One you can stand. Maybe even like. And what happens? You get fucked. I'm just calling it like I see it. He never calls. He calls all the time. He acts like you're invisible. He doesn't let you out of his sight for a minute. It's one thing or the other and no in-between. He vanishes or strangles. He fucks your sister. Whatever. In the end, who winds up miserable? Who winds up at home alone with the bad take-out and the laugh track? You. You. You. That's the thing that puts people in bell towers

.th high-powered rifles. The injustice of it. The men piss wherever they want and you gotta wash it off and try to get some business done. Have your heart broken and see if you wanna go to work. I look around me, at this world and these are the thoughts that come to me. I want to live in a world where everyone gets the shaft who deserves it and everyone gets ahead that works for it. I want an upright world. Half the world oppressed? Things don't spin right like that. Right?

(*He extends his hand.*)

I'm John.

MOTHER RUSSIA

Jeffrey Hatcher

McTeague, a oil company executive, in search of a big strike in Russia, remembers his youthful attempt to escape a mid-western orphanage, and why that failed attempt has cursed him to forever be in search of fuel.

McTEAGUE. Let me spell it out for you. The first time I drove a car I stole it. It was at The Our Lady of the Perpetual Mother of God Orphanage. I was thirteen years old, and I was gonna blow that midwestern pit if it took my last rites to do it. I was gonna steal a car and drive until I was outta the parking lot, out of the prairie, out all the way to I didn't care where, as long as there was money, booze, and women. I jimmied the lock on the door of my dorm, pried loose the wire from the windows, hopped the fence, broke into the head monk's car, and hot wired the ignition. It was a 1964 1/2 Mustang convertible. V-8 Cherry Red. Best thing America did after World War Two. I peeled back that top and roared that cherry down the interstate and never looked back…until about six miles out of town when I glanced down at the fuel gauge and saw that it was empty. And then I heard the sirens and the sound of that V-8 cool off, and I slowed to a stop. Cherry Red in the night, easiest thing in the world to see. And then they took me back for three more years of that stink-fingered priest-hole. From that night on, I vowed that I would never be without fuel again.

(He takes out a map and points.)

This spot. It's in a region called the Karkassas, 200 miles outside Moscow. Not much built on top. But below…below is the richest vein of oil I have ever seen. Six months ago I sent in a team of geologists, and the soil sample they sent back… Oooo, what I had to do to keep their mouths shut. This is a vein no one in the government knows about, no one in the whole oligarchy, not a single Russian...except for you. McTeague Oil has run companies all over the world: Texas, Abu Dabi, the North Sea. Nothing like Karkassas. McTeague Oil needs this land, but McTeague Oil can't *get* this land. Because McTeague is not Russian. After Communism collapsed, the land was privatized to the people who lived above it, and the law says they can't sell a majority interest to a foreigner. If any land is sold, a Russian must retain 51 per cent. I don't know who the owners are, but I'm driving there tomorrow. I need you to cast a spell. Protopopov says you are his best witch. Will you go there with me? I'm going to need you for things even I don't yet imagine.

A MURDER OF CROWS

Mac Wellman

Howard, along with his shouting wife, tries to disguise his disgust for his dead brother-in-law in order to give him a sad, proper eulogy.

HOWARD. You greedy old sows, fighting like swine over the dead, it's outrageous. We're a civilized people. Civilized people don't act this way. Civilized people would be acting like civilized people; civilized people would be saying sad things about the dead, like how worthy and noble they were, and how even if they never did much in life, and were pretty much a loser—a shiftless, untrustworthy, ne'er-do-well—, they still had a claim on our hearts. Even if they were like Raymond here, a total fizzle, a colossal existential dud, a complete and laughable failure at all he ever attempted in all his clownish, dipshit, clutzy life; he still was a HUMAN BEING and therefore worth a serious moment or so, on the occasion of his passing into the murk of the next world. One hell of crow's world where I fear he will be an object of much merriment among the angels and seraphim and hardbills.

(Pause. He laughs hysterically and starts up once more.)

But I confess I never thought much of him ever since we were boys together at high school in Horsedark, and he ratted on me when I looked over Jenny Miller's shoulder and got the answer right. He ratted and he ratted and he ratted on me, and I was humiliated in public. I never got over being humiliated in public, and I am a Christian gentleman so I believe in forgiveness and do not harbor grudges even though I'd like to gouge his eyes out of his head like jelly, because I may be a god-fearing American-type guy, a small-town, happy-go-lucky Christian-type fellow but you'd better remember I'm no wimp and if you fuck with me you will die and I don't never forget nothing nobody done did to me since I was ten

---

years old and this pathetic, crypto-commie, this alien stooge, this human farce; this rabbit-faced, luckless goon; this milksop; this weakling; this devious, evil-minded, dirty little yellow bastard;— man I wish I could've run him through a roaring buzzsaw, or chuck him wholehog into a MacCormick-Reaper and watch him spill out the other end like human spaghetti.

(Pause.)

But don't get me wrong, I loved the guy. I loved the son-of-a-gun. Why, when I think of all the things we done together I get the chills. Hay rides in the dark of the moon, baseball in the poison-ivy patch, harmless pranks on smaller, weaker, less entrepreneurly-minded kids, and so on and so forth; it makes me want to sit down and cry. He was the sweetest son-of-a-gun who ever soaked an anthill with kerosene and then tossed the lit match.

A MURDER OF CROWS

Mac Wellman

Raymond, who some say has died under a pile of radioactive chicken shit, punctures the shellac of the hollow age.

RAYMOND. Y the weather begets the heart's Y, I dunno. Some shall and some shall not and some all the more. Whole hills of wheat and no man shall slide low till what he love's above. Crows jerk and juke about and the winds wind up a medley of talkative hacksaws. We edge near the pit, back off, and think by baking apple pie we've got the key to the whole shitwagon and maybe we do. Maybe we don't, I'd love to know what the inside of a storm feels like to be one. I really do. But if it were up to me I'd skin the cat with a touch more care, seeing as how the consequences of what passes for luck at gin rummy, poker, and horses has a strange way of barking up the wrong tree.

(An avuncular pause.)

Now I know all this is probably stuff you've heard before, and from the wrong end of a television set, but I can't help wondering Y.

(A puzzled pause.)

I can't help wondering Y and I keep can't helping it, so help me, pigsfeet. The whole damn cross-eyed nest of squirrels keeps getting down on top of itself and going screwball. Now, let's just say for the sake of argument: you go and take a barrel of cheese all the way from Frankfurt, Kentucky clear to Cincinnati, a barrel of cheese disguised as a parrot, a barrel of cheese disguised as a pelican disguised as a flamingo. What it comes down to is this. What you've got is a case of the spirit of the age, which is not particularly understanding when it comes to strange feet, or love, or the simply enjoyment of a sunny day in middle of a bad winter. The spirit of the age's got its head wedged. The spirit of America sells used cars to unwary pedestrians, and they're all up on blocks. The cars, I mean. There's just a whole lot of old crap that would like to show itself to you. That would like to ask you a thing or two. A whole lot of cracker barrel horseshit that's trying to pass itself off as the bees-knees. A whole lot of beer-barrel hokum disguised as tragic corn-pone, a whole lot of small hurt disguised as big revenge, a whole lot of flag waving, and all of it, Y the weather, Y the whether or not, and it's all rolling up hill.

(Pause. He smiles.)

A MURDER OF CROWS

Mac Wellman

Andy, who up to this point was a mute golden statue, offers comfort to his mother.

ANDY. Hi Dad, hi Mom. Mom, I know you're in there.

(She [Mom] rises out of the coffin.)

I heard you talking about heaven so I thought you might want to hear about the real place. And it is a real place, just like hell, though neither one's in any book. I can see you've been concerned about me, but there's no reason to. I feel fine. I just don't have anything to say. The Gulf War was such a terrific high that I guess I've transcended a whole lot of lower human attributes. Things like doubt, fear, complexity, cat and dogs, girls. And since I've transcended knowledge and imagination too, I don't have a clue how this transpired. The truth is you don't need knowledge of human things or imagination where I am. And I know where heaven is, because that's where I am now. Really, and it's great. Heaven is like the Epcot Center or Disney World. Heaven is being inside the cockpit of an F14 on the approach to a nice, fat target in Baghdad. It's a feeling you can't describe and since you don't need to, why bother? "Bother" is another one of those words you don't need in heaven. Watching that smart bomb home in on the triple A, or parking ramp, or bridge, or command complex and the big blossom of golden flame darkening the morning all around me! That experience of bliss is like a medieval vision of Faith Rewarded—a pure act of wish come true. Somehow this experience has booted me up, up onto a whole, new plane of existence. I'm happy here. I have a bliss within that shines through me. You can see that I'm golden now. That's because I'm closer to god than you, and getting closer and closer. Inching nearer the holy flash point. See? I'm becoming a complete thing of gold. That's the mark of true beatitude. I am in touch with the wonders of metallization, velocity and pure kinetic being. Lots of my friends are with me. They all look like me. We're all happy. So don't worry about me. I'm doing great. It's just that I don't have anything to say to you, because I've gone way beyond where you are, which is fine with me. I never liked it down there anyway. I really look terrific, don't I? Beautiful skin is a gift from God, I guess.

MURMURING IN A DEAD TONGUE

J.T. Rogers

A Man sits before us in a chair, telling a fever-dream of a story: about a cock-tail party he's just come back from that went disastrously wrong, about channel-surfing between a mesmerizing surgery and the world's strangest action movie—and about the job that haunts him still.

MAN. I used to work at The Place. You know the one, the one everyone jokes about. Mystery Meat: where does it come from? Could be pig, yak, mongoose. You don't know. Nobody knows. You still go, you still put it in your mouth. Because everyone's a part of it. Eat there, work there, like a separate country, an empire unto itself, and I worked there and I'm not ashamed. I'm not proud, but I'm not ashamed. I lost my way. Just for a while. I wasn't focused, didn't understand my *potential*. And I would leave my car, I would walk towards the entrance, I would see the sign—Billions and Billions sold—and I would stand under the sky and grapple with that. What does that mean?

Billions.

Can you count that high?

Billions.

Try it. Add one number on top of another keeping a picture in your mind, an image of *what that number actually means*. Try it. Sixty-five. That's as far as I can get. I know, I know, not a record. I'm not ashamed. I'm not proud, but I'm not ashamed. I was haunted, haunted by that sign.

Billions sold.

Who sold them? What do they look like? What are their names? How many burgers were mine? What did I contribute? What was my worth? Because I was invisible, you see. I would stand in front of people, I would take their money, I would *give them food,* and they would look through me. I would stand there and I would heat and I would serve and I would talk to myself. (Oh, it's healthy, it's good, you should do it. Yes, yes, yes.) I would say:

"Why me? Why am I on this side?"

And the voice would say:
"Why do you think?"

"But I'm better. Don't you see? I'm better than them!"
'Well, honey, two points for you. So what?"
'My, my thoughts are sharp!"
"Un huh."
"They have a purpose!"
"Un huh."
"I have intelligence!"
"Wake up and smell the fruit pie, baby. Intelligence is irrelevant in America. You've got to do better than that."

And I would smile. I would stand behind that counter and I would think: *This world is fried. This world is deep fried.* And like a mantra it would come, it would sway through my body:

How do I live in a world in which I am doomed to die?
How do I live in a world in which I am doomed to die?
Would you like fries with that?
Maybe a shake?
You know, I made that burger.
That one's mine.

NATURAL SELECTION

Eric Coble

In the near future, domestic safari hunter Ernie is reporting back to his boss Henry about a failed attempt to bag a genuine native for the Culture Fiesta Theme Park.

ERNIE. So it's like the whole world's coming to an end, right? The chopper's entirely in flames now, right?

Debris everywhere, metal stalagmites jutting out of the black smoke, I look down and my entire arm is glittering—

A thousand shards of glass in my skin, I'm like a walking disco ball, a crystal porcupine—and I grab the two guides—one of 'em's screaming, the other's trying to scream, but he's just spitting out blood and gobs of flesh—

I throw 'em clear of the wreckage—twenty feet, I swear, I hurl this 180 pound man twenty feet—and the pilot—the pilot's out cold—probably 'cause her lower half has been ripped clean off—and I'm thinking, this is what I get for letting a woman drive! But I grab what's left of her and drag her out of the crash—and no sooner am I out of the ribs of the fuselage than BOOM!!

Reserve fuel tanks, whatever, BOOM!! I'm blown back thirty feet, face scorched, half my beard on fire—

But I'm already face down in the charred grass and rocks, I just rub my face in the ground— *(Demonstrates.)* BHHRRRHHRR—put out the flames—and I look around and I see, my god in heaven, some-how all of us—all of us—are still alive! So of course my thoughts go to the obvious question—

"Who's going to eat who first?"

Read this play at *www.playscripts.com*   87

We're miles from *anything*, Henry! We're out in the exposed air and light—we're one little helicopter—who's gonna come looking for us?

We were in the Adirondacks, Henry! Do you know anyone who's been to the Adirondacks since The Change?

I used to think the Montana—Texas Dust Belt was the most god-forsaken no-man's land on Earth, but I swear this whole continent, it's all gone to shit—and of course my gun's all twisted to hell, useless—my grandfather gave me that gun—

—graduation present—

Useless. Then I notice the heat from the chopper's inferno is actually melting the glass in my arm—I got liquid glass trickling down my wrist—

So I drip the glass onto the open wounds in the pilot and the one guide—it solidifies almost instantly, cauterizes the gaping veins and arteries—

We looked like stained glass pictures in Hell, Henry, I swear, sparkling with colors and textures man was not meant to see. And the smell—Jesus!

You can't guess. You weren't there, you never will be there, you will not try to impose your tiny little sensory imagination on my life.

You can't imagine the smell.

(Beat. ERNIE *stares hard at* HENRY.)

What we did have was a thirty story plume of black smoke and ash rising into the clear sky. I figured if we had any chance that was it. And I still had my knife— Strapped to my thigh like a second dick, my friend. I whipped that sucker out and started hacking down any and every piece of foliage I could—most everything was dead anyway—

—throwing it all on the fire, leaves, bark, birds, woodland animals, everything—

And they spotted us. Troop of Cub Scouts on one of their Extreme Wilderness Weekends—only group left dumb enough to leave the cities—

I was delirious with lack of blood, sleep, food—I could taste it— pure adrenaline in my mouth, my throat, feel it pulsing behind my eyes—you ever tasted the secretion of your own adrenal glands?

Pray you never do. Tastes like mud, like the primordial ooze we crawled out of, mixed with blood and semen.

I guess I didn't stop when the Scout troop showed up, kept carving, kept moving, kept swearing—apparently I took out two kids trying for a wolf badge in first aid.

But the point is—and I don't think this was lost on the Cub pack—I survived. I looked right into the jaws of the oblivion beast, that dread maw of eternal night, and I said—not for the first time either—"Fuck You."

NEVER TELL

James Christy

Hoover is a 14 year old slacker, recounting his first wet dream. The speech is part of a flashback and should be performed by an adult (in the play Hoover is in his early 30s).

HOOVER. So I'm in this office, this really cool office. And I realize it's like a record company office, with gold records and shit all around. And I'm a big-shot record executive. And it's like I can do anything I want. Anything. I can call famous musicians or hook up with girls, whatever I want. So I'm sitting there deciding what I want to do, and Bob Marley walks in. Bob Marley. Now my dad played me Bob Marley records ever since I was like a baby so I know how big this is. But before I can think of anything to say he starts yelling at me and saying how I screwed him out of all this money in some record deal. And I'm trying to tell him no, you know, it isn't me, this isn't really my office, I'm just sitting here. But I can't get it out, I can't even talk. And he just keeps coming closer, behind the desk to where I'm sitting and right in front of me and I'm so scared. But at the same time, you know, I can't stop thinking how cool it is that he's talking to me. I also kind of knew in the back of my mind that he's dead, but that just made it that much cooler. So just as I'm starting to get scared that he's really going to fuck me up, I look down and I realize that I have this huge boner. And it freaks me out because I know you're not supposed to get boners in front of guys and it might make him even madder, but it's just happening and I can't do anything about it. So he looks down and he sees my boner, and he sort of smiles and stops being mad. Like he realizes he has the wrong guy. So then he just turns around and walks out. So that was it, that was my first time. Bob Marley.

NEVER TELL

James Christy

Manny is a shy 14 year old, describing the events surround his father's suicide the previous fall. The speech is part of a flashback and should be performed by an adult (in the play Manny is in his late 20s).

MANNY. I figured it out last year. Right after my 13th birthday. That's too old, I know. I had been hearing about it for a while. Not anything specific, just that there was something you could do, you know? By yourself. And it was dirty. And I wanted to, you know. I had seen dirty magazines at my cousin's house, and I wanted to follow along and be just as dirty as anyone else. But I just didn't know what exactly I was supposed to do. I knew something needed to happen to it, and I'd look at it and wonder what the hell it could be. I thought it had to be some kind of procedure, with equipment and instructions and all. Finally I was in the shower one morning and it just happened. And I guess I was relieved at first. But afterwards I got out and went into my room, and I felt so stupid. Like, how come everyone else figured this out and I couldn't? What's so different about me? It's like there's something natural that everybody gets that I missed. And I sat on my bed thinking that I'd never figure out what it was. Finally my mother called me and made me go to school. But after second period the principal took me out of class and drove me home. He drove me himself. I thought he found out somehow what I'd done in the shower. It turned out my dad had hung himself in the garage during the night.

(Beat.)

And sometimes I think about it when I'm doing that. That the first time I did it my dad was hanging there in the garage. And I wonder like I wondered that morning in my room what it was I missed.

NEVER TELL

James Christy

Will is a cocky 14 year old bragging about a public sexual conquest from the 8th grade. The speech is part of a flashback and should be performed by an adult (in the play Will is in his late 20s).

WILL. The whole school was talking about it for weeks. I was like a celebrity. I could tell even while it was happening. All the boys looked at me like I was a rock star, the girls just looked terrified. But interested... It was last spring in 7th grade. Michelle started riding our bus after Christmas, and she would always sit next to me in the last row of the bus. She was in 10th grade and usually 10th grade girls are chasing seniors, not 7th graders. But she'd sit there with me and ask me these questions. About what girlfriends I've had, what I've done with them. But the main thing was that when she was talking to me she'd put her hand on my leg and sort of rub it there. And the further on we got in the year the farther she got up my leg. Until one morning she actually unzipped my fly, put her bookbag over my lap, and did it to me with her hand. Right there on the back of bus 33. It was so cool. There was something about doing that in front of everyone, seeing their faces. Especially the girls. I can't explain it. I've had real sex now, but it wasn't as good as that. I don't know if it's ever going to be as good as that.

THE NEW FIRE

Paul Grellong

Nick Reed is a tightly wound guy who just got fired. He wants his job back more than anything in the world, so he runs off at the mouth in a desperate attempt to reason with Mr. Heyworth, his former boss.

NICK. I don't think it's too late for us to talk about this. Sir? Let me just begin by saying that: *sir.* It's not too late.

> *(Pause.)*

Would it be too forward of me to sit down? To sit right down next to you?

> *(No response.)*

Okay, I'm here because of these…special circumstances between us. Because of the kind of morning we've had…it was such a hard morning…so, given these special and hard circumstances I'm going to take your silence in response to the me-sitting-down question as a kind of "non-verbal yes." I am "getting to yes" here. I'll ask one more time and take your response, whatever it may be, at face value. Remember, though, that silence will be taken to mean "yes." It will mean, "please sit down." All right. Sir. Sir? May I sit down? May I sit down next to you?

> *(No response.)*

Thank you, sir.

> *(NICK sits down on the bench. A cardboard box rests awkwardly on his lap.)*

The way I see it, *two* reasons it makes sense to give me back my job. "I'm a hard worker," yes, but that's only one. And, yes, I *am* a hard worker, but the second is, sir, "this is all a big misunderstanding."

And we'll get to that, we really will. But I truly do believe that we can put this morning's ugliness and pain behind us.

(Pause.)

God…it was ugly. And I found it painful. What about you? Do you remember that? Earlier this morning, in your office? I'm thinking about it now, I'm like: *whoa.* What a scene, you know? I'm sorry that I cried. I wept like a little girl and that was wrong. But it's what I was feeling!

(Pause.)

A lot of people cry when they are confused. I do. Also when they're sad. When do you cry? I don't know. You seem really strong. Like a big wall or a…huge…thick-skinned creature from another age. Does that make sense, sir? You seem *brave*, I don't know if you cry at all. But I mostly cry when I'm confused, which I most certainly was when I was informed this morning of my dismissal from the company. In this case, certainly I was sad as well, so that was like a combo-cry.

What is "being fired"? What is "downsizing"? What does it mean to be "downsized"? I've been thinking about this for just under an hour now. What are these things? What do they mean?

(Pause.)

Obviously, their short term meaning is pretty clear. "Leave the building." "Leave the building now or we will call security." "Hello, I'm *from* security, follow me." And they put you in the elevator. Then you're standing outside. Holding a cardboard box. Like this one. I'm going to put this down now if that's all right.

(NICK leans over and places the cardboard box on the ground by his feet.)

You know, a lot of people say, and I'm sure you've heard this, boss, they say, "Oh, hey, listen, I never bring my work home with me." Mentally, they mean this. Well, me? I'll go you one better. I never bring my *home* to work with me, you know, despite the mis—the incorrect things in the report that you got, that you read. By that I mean that whatever problems might or might not be happening on the home front, they *stay* on the home front. Like: Sandra and I broke up last week. Sure. Did I bring that to the office with me? *I would never do that.* I mean, there was nothing to bring, a la per se, it was a mutual decision. As far as breakups go, it was a…it was very good. An amicable split that's not at all contributing to…to what we're talking about here, which is a job. My job. My *old* job. And making it my new job. Again.

    (Pause.)

But what of those questions I posed? How can you and I discuss the viability of, say, a rehire situation when we haven't first wrestled with and wrapped our minds around the culture of firing, of downsizing? What does it mean for individuals? What does it mean for the country? There are so many questions. What exactly is a "layoff"? What is "inappropriate use of office materials"? What, furthermore, is the sense in a situation where one is "downsized" and escorted to the elevator by security and that woman from Human Resources? I think it's bad for the company, sir. That's the case I'm here to make with you this morning. That the company, and you personally, are better off with me than without me.

PEER GYNT

adapted by David Henry Hwang and Stephan Müller
based on the play by Henrik Ibsen

Peer, who was supposed to have brought a deer home to his mother, attempts to justify how he destroyed his clothes, lost his gun, and came home meatless.

PEER. The blizzard so strong, I was fighting off sleep. The sleep of death. Then I saw—brown—a hoof—pawing at green—some moss.

And blood starts to pump back into my brain. I hear scraping, see the razor-sharp tips of his antlers. Feel myself moving—on my belly, through the thick white curtain. And then I see him—all of him, like a vision—the perfect buck—so tall and fat.

Kablam! My gun fires! Whomp! He goes down. Now *I'm* the animal—leaping onto his back. Grabbing his left ear—got'cha! My knife, poised in midair, ready to strike his neck with the finishing blow…

> *(Pause.)*

Oh, God! Mother! He bellows! And leaps onto his feet. Rearing up on his hind legs, flinging my knife out of my reach! Before I can think, his antlers, they're pinning my hips—Jesus, the pain!—squeezing me, like a vice, against his body. I'm thrashing helplessly, a rag-doll. Both of us still in this position, he jumps up, then takes off along the ridge of Gjendin!

A sheer drop, one—no, three, five thousand feet into oblivion. Just as I start to gather my wits—squawk! A wild rooster explodes from a cave, feathers everywhere, blinding the beast. The buck, startled, leaps off into…into…

Into thin air! We're falling straight down, plummeting through the abyss. Above us, sheer rock wall zooming by. Beneath us, certain

Actor's Choice: Monologues for Men

annihilation. Falling through a curtain of clouds, even parting a flock of seagulls! And still we continue—down, down—until, what's that coming towards us from beneath? It looks...like a reindeer's belly. Mother, I was seeing our reflection, in the waters below, rushing towards the horrible collision!

Buck above, buck below—crash into each other, kicking up icy waters, vomiting foam. Both of us still struggling, scratching— barely conscious. Until somehow, we find ourselves heading for shore.

    (Pause.)

And now, can you believe it? Here I am.

PERMANENT COLLECTION

Thomas Gibbons

Sterling North, a successful African-American businessman, has been appointed the new director of the Morris Foundation, a world-famous collection of Impressionist art. In this opening monologue he describes an encounter with a police officer as he drives to the Foundation on his first day.

STERLING. Put yourself in my place.

You're driving along Spencer Avenue on your way to the Foundation. It's a glorious day—sun shining, trees blazing with autumn color, and you're in your favorite car. You pass a 7-Eleven and see a police cruiser waiting to pull out of the parking lot. And no sooner does the thought appear in your mind, the acknowledgment that it's been a while for you, quite a while in fact, and that you are not just due but overdue—no sooner does the thought exist than you hear the bleat of his siren and see his lights dancing in your rear-view mirror.

All right, you think, the universe has decided to give you one of its periodic reminders, and it is today. This day of all days. You pull over and watch the cop get out of his car. A corner of your mind automatically runs down the checklist—the one your father drummed into you and that you've drummed into your own son. Your daughter as well, of course, but especially your son because he's just turned seventeen, that dangerous age when feeling is quicker than intellect. Keep your hands in sight, don't make any unexpected movements, address him as "Officer."

You roll down your window. "Is there a problem, officer?" you say. Of course you know what the problem is—DWB—but there's a script to be followed in these encounters and you are following it. "Is this your car, sir?" he asks. Of course you know what he's thinking: You're a prize specimen—a black man in a Jag. And behind that question is a series of other questions he wants to ask, the real questions: Is that your suit? Are those your handlasted English shoes? Is this your *life*? But he's sticking to the script too. "Yes, it is," you say. "May I see your registration, please?" "Certainly," you reply, and reach into your pocket—slowly, of course; this is the first moment when the index of danger ticks upward. You take out your wallet and hand him the card. He studies it for a moment, then says, "May I ask where you're going, sir?"

You're about to answer when a feeling comes over you, a feeling of— *(For a moment he is, uncharacteristically, at a loss for words.)* Indignation? No, not that, or not *only* that—it's there, certainly, but mixed with something else: the realization of where you are going, yes, and what that means. The triumph it represents. It's a dangerous feeling, you recognize immediately, a feeling to be resisted. But it sweeps across the barrier of your caution like an overpowering flood. And you decide that today, on this day of all days, you are going to depart from the script.

"Well, Officer," you say, "the fact is, legally, you don't have the right to ask me where I'm going." Behind his green sunglasses his eyes narrow—you can't see them, of course, but you don't have to, you sense it, this guy is *transparent* to you. "But because this is a special day, I'll answer your question. I'm going to the Morris Foundation on Church Lane. You've heard of the Morris, I'm sure, but perhaps you've never been there. It's one of the largest, most important collections of Impressionist art in the world—right here in your own back yard. And the reason I'm going there is that I've just been appointed its new director. So you'll be seeing my car quite often. Now, Officer, what I would like you to do is this. I'd like you to go back to the station and put a description of this car on the bulletin board. Burgundy 2003 Jaguar, license number ARY-3427. Make sure all of your fellow officers see it. Tell them to *memorize* it. Because the next cop who pulls me over for being black is going to have his ass sued for a truly staggering amount of money." You hold out your hand. "May I have my registration, please?"

Oh, it's sweet. Stupid too, you realize. Unfathomably stupid. If your son told you he had done anything like this, you would—

(Pause.)

The cop stands there, studying you, and you recognize the look on his face. The same look you would see on the faces of other executives in the company—white executives—early in your career. The dismaying realization that they'd underestimated you, badly, and now they found themselves standing still while you moved up. You can hear the questions running through the cop's mind as clearly as if he's thinking out loud. He's never heard of the Morris Foundation—could you be telling the truth? You obviously have money; are you politically connected? Can you hurt him with a well-placed phone call? Are you a *lawyer?*

You've reached the moment you love—the telling moment when it becomes clear who's won and who's lost. He'll ask you to step out of the car—not to handcuff you; after all, you haven't *done* anything—but to spreadeagle you on the hood and pat you down, a roadside display of humiliation. Or he'll give you back your registration card and go on his way. Later on, over a beer in the cops' favorite bar or maybe in someone's basement, somewhere *safe*, he'll tell his buddies about the uppity nigger he stopped today. Or he'll say nothing. Nothing at all.

You watch his face, and— *(He snaps his fingers.)* —you see the decision. Without a word he hands you the card, walks back to his cruiser, and drives off.

You sit for a moment, regrouping, then you go on your way. Down the quiet, tree-lined streets of Ridgewood, past the old, expensive houses regarding you from behind their emerald lawns, and through the gate of the Foundation. You park and walk up the marble steps to the huge oak door.

(A moment, then he picks up a box.)

Yes, that is my car.

This is my suit.

These are my shoes.

This is my life.

POST-OEDIPUS

Steven Gridley

Oedipus, old and blind, attempts to eulogize his two sons, Eteocles and Poly-neices, who just killed each other in an attempt to gain control over Thebes, Oedipus' old kingdom. Jocasta, his wife, ignores him, as she always does.

OEDIPUS. As father of these two, and Ismene, and former king of Thebes, I feel like I should say a few things. Thank you. Thank you. A father's love... A father's love... A father's love... We will remember these days always won't we? Why am I still alive? I think I should have died a long time ago. Jocasta? Can you remember? It was not always this way. All my dreams are about to descend upon me, Antigone. I finally realize now...dreams don't come to you. You wait and wait but the damn dreams won't come! You have to go to them. You have to go to sleep. That's the only way. So I'm going. And I hope... I hope my first dream is the story of my re-turn. My return to glory. The power of Thebes will return to my chest. My hands and feet will regain their strength. They will, Anti-gone. And I will retake what was mine. Everything. It all will come back. And the whole kingdom will remember me. And then...once I have regained my power and reclaimed my throne, and I have returned to my full stature, and people praise my name once more...then Jocasta, yes, even Jocasta will come back to me and bend her knee and bow her head and beg that I forgive her long absence and ask that I look beyond her long silence, and she will Wet My Feet With Her Tears. And I will look down on her with hard eyes and a closed fist and with my hard eyes and closed fist I will say, "I forgive you. I'll always forgive you."

The Potato Creek Chair of Death

Robert Kerr

Michael is a teenage fugitive from Ohio seeking a legendary "chair of death." In this monologue, he confesses to Valerie, an elderly woman with whom he has forged a connection, why he is on the run from the law.

MICHAEL. Finding you wasn't part of the plan.

No. I don't mean that. You must have been a part of the plan I didn't know about. The plan for my life. What I'm meant to do. I feel like I'm reading the signs all wrong. It wasn't me that killed my parents, right? It was the universe. I was just a tool. They were meant to die. I just did what the signs said I should do.

I mean, when I got up at two in the morning and I was really thirsty so I went downstairs and I was looking for the orange juice pitcher, it was a sign when I opened the cupboard where Mom kept the rat poison. I wasn't thinking about it. I just opened it by mistake. Except it wasn't a mistake because the universe does things like that gets in your brain and makes you do things. I didn't know right away what I should do with the poison. But I knew it was either them or me.

I had to make sure I did the right thing, so I made the orange juice and poured it into two cups that looked exactly the same and put the poison in one of them. I closed my eyes and switched them around a bunch of times and spun myself around so I was really dizzy. I kept my eyes closed and took one of the cups and drank it. I felt kind of sick, but I didn't know if I drank the one with the poison so I poured the other cup back into the pitcher and went to bed.

I couldn't fall asleep right away, but I didn't feel as sick after a while. Then I thought maybe I should tell my parents about the poison. But it was like too much trouble to get them up at three in the morning. I turned off the alarm because if I woke up on my own in time I was meant to save their lives.

I fell asleep and I dreamed about the Chair of Death which I heard about in second grade. I woke up and I wasn't... So they were.... I got the car. I started driving. I knew I had to find the Chair of Death because I had that dream about it. And now I feel like I'm Charles Manson or something, because I guess compared to other parents mine weren't all that bad. They never hit me. They never grabbed for my crotch. They never did anything. I never did anything. We all just sat around doing nothing. It was like we were all already dead, so what difference does it make if I really did kill them, right?

PRIDE AND PREJUDICE

adapted by Jon Jory
from the novel by Jane Austen

Hertfordshire, England, 1813. Darcy, a wealthy landowner, professes his love to Elizabeth, explaining why he's he has hid his true feelings.

DARCY. In vain have I struggled. It will not do. My feelings will not be repressed. You must allow me to tell you how ardently I admire and love you.

I see I dismay you. I am slow, even dilatory. I should have declared myself at an earlier date. But there were, of course, the family obstacles which judgment always opposed to inclination. The general sense of your social inferiority, of it being a degradation of the line. I could not forget my responsibility to an estate, a way of life, a pride of place which might given your circumstances disinclude you and thus the very ardency I described took place against my will and reason, or rather in opposition to my character and inclination, but the very strength of my attachment has made it impossible for me to conquer my feelings and I can only express the hope that these feelings will now be rewarded by your acceptance of my hand. There.

I have spoken ill but mean well, Miss Bennet.

PROCLIVITIES

Kirsten Greenidge

After being harassed by a street peddler supposedly selling chocolates for a good cause, Doug finally snaps. He rants about the reasons he's entitled to spend his money however he sees fit, especially given how hard he's worked.

DOUG. I only have cards. What does that tell you? I paid for this organic four dollar and thirty nine cent spread that my doctor says I need and my wife says I need but I don't think I need but I want to trust my doctor but I'm not so sure about my wife, but I should really trust my doctor because I don't want to die I'm too young to die but maybe that would be better maybe that would be best because I'm paying for my groceries my *groceries* with credit because I don't have any, with the car loan and the mortgage I'm not even thirty and I have a *mortgage* it's a good neighborhood, it's a very good school system, there aren't even any chain stores, not a one, not even a McDonalds so I'm leaking I'm just *leaking* checks that will probably bounce, I'm leaking my savings my parents have savings but I don't have savings I don't have anything it's all plastic it's all electronic which isn't fair, I don't think it's fair, because you grow up, you grow up and you're surrounded by all the things you know should be yours when you're older, that show you've worked and you're here, you're *here*, you're a member, a productive member, of society, and you should be like your parents, you should have vacuum cleaners and hammocks to put your fruit in your kitchen that has every appliance a kitchen with marble counter tops is supposed to have and I don't think those things should be denied to me, they're my birthright, and so I say forget it: I say I can't worry about helmets and buckets because if I want spread that costs four *hundred* dollars and thirty nine cents I'm entitled. Shouldn't I be entitled?

THE REDEEMER

Cybèle May

Stewart, a detective, attempts to open up to his female partner, but ends up making an uncomfortable confession.

STEWART. I can't go home. I can't sleep there. I keep having this dream.

(Pause.)

I'm at camp… I think I'm a kid. The kids are out in the river on a swimming platform. They're yelling for me, waving me out. I'm running back and forth along the shore, like a dog does, you know. The rocks are slimy and I keep slipping and my mother's made me wear these little canvas sneakers because she was afraid of broken glass and snapping turtles.

(Pause. He tries to remember.)

Suddenly I'm swimming out to them. The water is cold, and it's over my head and I feel the weeds pulling at my feet… The current is washing me downstream and the more I kick the more my feet get tangled. I panic and I swallow water and I'm kicking and my legs are hurting…the kids are screaming now.

(Pause.)

I get to the platform and pull myself up and…and…I'm in the big lodge now. It's this huge room with tall ceilings with exposed beams. The kids are gone and it's really quiet. There are these big birds all over the place, hopping around on the furniture and the tables. Kind of like crows, glossy black with red beaks. …One starts pecking at my hand, at first just lightly. I put my hands in my pockets, but the other birds hop over their claws ticking on the wood.

(Pause.)

They're all pulling and tearing at my pants to get at my hands… I pick up the first bird in front of me by the legs and I start swinging him to get the other ones away. The one in my hands, he doesn't seem to want to get away, he's just calmly biting my hands. I slam him against a table and he keeps doing it, I slam him against the wall…over and over again until he is limp in my hands and his feathers are wet and sticky. I drop him to the floor.

(Long silence.)

I'm not asking you to tell me what it means.

(Pause.)

I guess I should leave. I'm sorry. I shouldn't have…no, I gotta go.

Actor's Choice: Monologues for Men

THE REDEEMER

Cybèle May

Stewart, a detective driven to the edge, returns from a failed attempt to retrieve a kidnapped boy, and makes an unusual confession.

STEWART. It was an accident.

(*Pause.*)

We were in the car. We were running late. She was supposed to have hemmed the pants of my suit. She hadn't only I didn't know until I put 'em on so I had to keep them up with masking tape. It looked terrible but she kept saying that we were going to be late. So we were in the car and she looked down at me and said I looked ridiculous and she was glad that she had no standards left otherwise she would be humiliated to be seen with me. That's when I started yelling—what did she want from me? She wanted me to lose control, didn't she? And then she started laughing. The faster I drove the funnier I was and the louder she laughed. I couldn't take it, I couldn't take any of it anymore. We were ugly. I wanted both of us dead. Suddenly, I wanted it all to be over and I turned straight into the oncoming traffic.

(*Pause.*)

I forgot Tommy was in the back. I forgot my boy was there. He was all dressed up in his little blue suit. If it hadn't been so messed up in the accident he would have been buried in it. He was so quiet, quiet all the time. Shiny black hair, brown eyes. He had freckles from playing soccer all summer with the neighbor kid in the yard. He'd curl up on my lap and put his face against my chest and tap along with my heart. We used to eat cereal for supper when his mother wasn't home.

(*Pause.*)

I told everyone it was my fault. They'd just hug me and say it would be okay and that I'd stop blaming myself someday. They didn't realize that I had actually done it, it really was my fault.

SECRET THINGS

Elaine Romero

After a bitter fight with a female journalist (Delia) who has been interviewing him about his claim of Mexican-Jewish roots, Abel visits his Rabbi and offers his confession.

ABEL. No. But she's Jewish. I mean, I did her family history. I mean, she doesn't even know she is, so I guess she's not. I don't know what it means.

I've never told you. About my past. I slept with so many women. I honestly don't know how many. And I feel very bad. I hurt a lot of feelings. I feel that was wrong. I feel a little messed up over it, frankly.

And I, uh, had this commitment. To myself. When we did the Rite to Return. To not do that anymore. I mean, to let the floodgates open up again. I just don't know what would happen. So, I haven't done anything. I just closed myself off. And I want to find the proper way to be open again and I just can't. I just feel this fear— this block. I don't know. Maybe I want the next woman I make love to to be my wife. Would that be crazy?

I mean, me and this woman are nowhere near having sex. I mean, we haven't even kissed. We haven't even held hands. We've barely talked. And she's threatened to never talk to me again.

But I think she really really likes me, and I most definitely like her, and I, uh, would like to get to know her better. Um, she's really really sharp. And I really really like that. I mean, I feel so alive. I mean, like when we're talking we're both really thinking hard. And I love that. Because when you're old. When you're really really old—that might be all that's left—is somebody you can think with. Somebody who can share your thoughts. And finish your sentences. And laugh at your stupid jokes. And still find you attractive

---

when you are not remotely attractive at all. Because they've found a way to peer into your soul. And they like it.

Am I asking too much?

SECRET THINGS

Elaine Romero

Delia, a native New Mexican journalist who lives in New York, has returned to New Mexico to debunk the claims of local New Mexicans that they have Jewish roots. She is disarmed when Abel shares his personal experience of observing Jewish practices in his New Mexican Catholic home.

ABEL. These memories kept flashing back at me. Images I couldn't explain away. I remember my mother and grandmother, locking themselves in the closet on Friday nights. And that muffled sound of the Hebrew language—it was like nothing I'd ever heard before. Frightening, actually. It always started with Baruka-something. I remember cracking the door open one time when they were praying and seeing the red glow of wine against the candlelight. It was beautiful. The light reflecting off their faces as they swept the light into themselves with their hands. And their expressions—entranced by God, I suppose. When I asked my mother about it later, she ignored me. When I pressed her further, she said she and my grandmother were having a private conversation—a private conversation in a language I couldn't understand. "What were you saying?" I asked. What were you saying?" I could tell in that moment that she wanted to tell me—the words were stuck in her heart, trying to find a way to her lips, but I was on the verge of making my Catholic confirmation the next week and she stubbornly didn't want to deter me from the path she had picked for me. She didn't have faith that I could comprehend her contradiction that she was a Catholic on the outside and a Jew on the inside. Fridays never felt the same after that. Me and my mother never felt the same after that as this secret grew between us like a cement wall between two fragile hearts. All she needed to say was, "I am observing Shabbat." I would have looked into it myself. I've always been a very curious person. Even when I was a little kid. I would have started observing Shabbat on my own. I did, actually, one time with grape juice and a match. I don't know why I'm telling you this.

SPLIT

Allison Moore

Brock, a sweet, laid-back skateboarder in his late 20s, has just surprised his best friend, Kit, by replacing her broken toilet. She insists on paying him back for the toilet. In refusing to take her money he is forced to confess how he feels about her.

BROCK. I mean, I've been working at Daeco since I was in college. And you've seen my place, what do I spend money on? I don't even have any student loans. I actually have kind of a lot saved up. And I've been thinking about what I want to do. I know it seems like I'm kind of aimless, I know your dad thinks that, anyway, and I'm definitely still figuring it all out, but. I am so *not bored.* And a lot of people are. It kinda blows me away, because, I mean, I love skating, and hanging with my friends, and— I know I'm more of a listener than a talker, but, that's because I'm interested in other people. What they get worked up about, or pretend they don't care about, but you can tell, you know, that they really do—I totally do that with you. And even some of the people at Daeco, you know? They are some interesting people there. The job itself is kind of repetitive, and I don't want to do it forever, but. It gives me a lot of time to think, and. One of the things I've been thinking about for awhile is. Buying a house? Because I've definitely got enough for down payment and all that. And that got me to thinking that maybe instead of, you know, house shopping, maybe I could, um. Buy Jake's half. Of this house. And then you wouldn't have to move, and Jake could get his own place like he wants, and if your dad gets better he can come back, and, and I would, you know. Live here. With you. If that's something you would want.

STILL LIFE

Seth Kramer

David, fellow survivor, admits to his downstairs neighbor that he used to secretly watch her paint before their building was destroyed in a fire. He uses his revelation to try and help her recover the desire to paint again.

DAVID. Do you know, before I ever even talked to you I was memorizing your artwork. Did you know that?

(Beat.)

I've never had the courage to tell you this before.

(Beat.)

I used—I'd go onto my fire escape to have a smoke. I'd do it after coming home from work, when it was late, even during the winter. I just liked to have a place to go and sit and be by myself. I'd always...always hear your music playing at two something in the morning. Always some jazz or fusion thing coming from your window. After a few months—I was curious. So, I...one day... One day, instead of just sitting there, I climbed down the two floors between us and peeked in. Into your studio. You were working on a painting of yourself. I still remember. A black and white contour image. You had this light set to cast shadows over yourself and were working from a mirror. I sat there all night with you. Watching. Afraid to stay because you might notice me. Unable to leave because I didn't want to miss anything.

(Pause.)

After that...after that I couldn't stay away. I'd look forward to what new thing I might see every few days. Something as it was created there on your stand. I was giddy—God I can't believe I am telling you this—giddy when I saw a new blank canvas set up. The anticipation of what you might make next.

(Pause.)

That was you. That's what drew me to you. Not the art itself—although it was amazing—but the act of creating. That passion.

(Pause.)

Eight months ago, when all this happened, when our building caught on fire, I didn't think life could get any worse. I questioned everything. Why it happened, how it started. All that. I don't know if I was supposed learn something from the experience or if I'll ever understand it. All I know is…what it cost. In the span of a few hours every single thing I owned was reduced to ashes. Books, clothes, computers, music, photographs, all of it. It was difficult to watch but those were just things. Just objects.

(Beat.)

When I saw you run into the building I knew what you were going to do so I followed. I know you hate me for doing what I did. For dragging you out like that, but I couldn't let you…

(Beat.)

There was no way to save the paintings.

(Pause.)

Please…don't let this fire destroy everything you still have left to create too.

THEATER DISTRICT

Richard Kramer

George Bridge explains to Wesley, his partner's teenaged son, how he knew for the first time he was gay.

GEORGE. *(To stop him:)* —You asked me a question this morning, Wesley. Before the day turned into—*today*. Remember? You asked me—among other things—how I knew. So.

> *(A beat. GEORGE breathes. Then, slowly, he is filled with the answer to* WESLEY's *early morning question:)*

So I would take the train. To the city. I was your age, about. Wednesdays, I'd cut school, get a half-price ticket to something, anything, it didn't matter what. Then one day—I actually get into—A CHORUS LINE…

Standing room. And there they are, with their pictures in front of their faces… And there's this guy.

> *(A beat.)*

Standing. Next to me. Around my age… Then the pictures drop, and you see their faces—

> *(He sings.)*

"Who am I anyway… Am I my resume…"

> *(A beat.)*

We're both leaning on our stuff, on the ledge, our coats and scarves. He never looks at me, I never look at him, but there's music and right behind us these tiny Irish ladies with flashlights, and lace—and his hand touches mine. Under the coats…

> *(A beat.)*

Then—he slips a ring from his finger onto mine. That's all. And it stays there, till the end. We just keep looking forward, until everyone stands and cheers—

(*A beat, as he shuts his eyes, touches his ring finger, hears the cheers once more. He's almost lost in that until—*)

Then I say— "I'm George…"

(*After a moment:*) "I'm George, too."

(*A beat.*)

And he's gone. It wasn't until supper that night… I was telling some lie about school that day, I was cutting a pork chop and I saw—

I still had the ring.

THROW PITCHFORK

Alexander Thomas

Jimmy, a hard core drug addict, attempts to defend and rationalize his drug addicted behavior to a counselor (and/or drug counseling peer group).

JIMMY. *(Lanky, dangling arms and fingers, head turning from side to side like some nervous radar.)* I'm an addict. A junkie. I admit that. I admit that. I get sick and tired of people talking; "Look at Jimmy. Jimmy is the oldest one. Jimmy's suppose to be the big brother—he messin' up. Jimmy's supposed to help his little brothers—he runnin' the streets. Jimmy's supposed to set an example—he shootin' dope. He dippin' 'n' dabbin', he sellin' 'n' dealing, he boostin' 'n' stealin'. Hey, I'm *gonna do some horse!* I admit that. I'm gonna boast a little, steal a little. But at least I admit it. I'll take something from you but it's to feed my habit. It's not malicious. It's not to do you harm. I ain't never hurt nobody. And I'm gonna always, as soon I can, pay it back. You will git your shit back soon as I can. So I don't really see what the problem is. I know it's wrong but I admit that. I tried to stop. I been to treatment programs 'n' things. Shit don't work for me. All the lingo: I got a "disease," an "obsession," a "compulsion." I gotta "arrest it a day at a time." I got "enablers." Come from a "dysfunctional family." Now, that's true! That's true. This family? Like, just put your self in this situation. Just imagine this. Let's say you got a brother that you know is a junkie, an addict. Now, you know that this brother has been messin' around shootin' up since he was what, 17, 18 maybe even younger. Now just imagine this. You let this brother stay at your house. Now, you know he's been known to steal, borrow, whatever from time to time when he needs to get high. Now, you leave a credit card laying around. A credit card! It's not in your purse, not in your wallet, not in drawer. Nowhere. No normal safe place. It's on the table. Just laying on the table! He takes and uses it. Any junkie would do this,

right? Now, would you call the police on your own blood? See…
"Dysfunctional!" Call the police on your own blood. I'm not sayin'
I'm not wrong. I am wrong, I am wrong, I am wrong. I admit that.
All I'm sayin' is I get sick and tired, and I'm sick and tired of being
sick and tired, of this family doing stupid shit and then blame it on
me when I'm just being an addict. A junkie, that's all. And that, I
admit.

TO MOSCOW!

Jeanmarie Williams

A History Teacher addresses his students, quashing their imaginative minds with a very conservative view of the universe.

HISTORY TEACHER. And so we find, of course, that Time is a line. Time, as we know, as we've all *suspected* for millions of years, is a line with two points that stretch out on into Infinity—now there's a word—Infinity, until Time will stop, which of course, we know it will not.

The religious among you may ask, yes, but what about God? What about that glorious first moment and the inevitable last? I offer for your consideration the idea that, truth be told, yes, that this book you read with such fervor and passion, is not a map, no, a violent *tool*, perhaps, but definitely, merely, at last, a guide. And that's all I have to say about that.

Now some of you are thinking something right now, wandering off as it were, seeing visions of circles and continuumzzz of your own, constructing little epi-sssodes and intrigues, perhaps about some alternative geometric theory, some loop that folds back onto itself. And maverick though you be, I tell you this. You are also wrong.

Think about yesterday and then consider today. Imagine tomorrow. Buck up. You are not lost. You can find yourself if you place yourself on the line. Get in line, little soldiers, get in line. Get in line and look to the right. Look ahead. See yourself on the line. Where are you going? Where will you end up? On the line. Where have you been? What have you done? Look to the left. See yourself there as you were. You've been on the line this whole time.

I know this is comforting to you. It's comforting to me as well. Can we ask any more from History? Can we ask for any more comfort than this?

TRUMBO:
RED, WHITE & BLACKLISTED

Christopher Trumbo

The Narrator reveals how his father, the screenwriter Dalton Trumbo, taught him about communism and capitalism.

NARRATOR. Early on, my parents decided that they would be as truthful as possible with my sisters and me. There would be no secrets—not about our situation, the possibility of jail, about politics, or work. They told us to ask any questions we wanted. My sister Nicky was 11, I was 9. Mitzi, only 4, wasn't ready for these family briefings.

Nicky and I wanted to know about communism. It was explained to us that communism was a system where people were provided for on the basis of "from each according to his ability to each according to his needs." Capitalism was explained as a system where one person hires a second person to perform some task and then sells the product to a third person for profit.

From politics we moved on to the idea of God and the major religions.

At the end of this session my sister stoutly declared that when she grew up she would be a communist and a Jew. More modestly, I expressed a desire to become a capitalist and a Catholic.

Tumor

Sheila Callaghan

Richard reminisces about his spur-of-the-moment marriage to Kathy and confesses to his growing apprehensions about having a baby, especially when they already have enough trouble taking care of their pet dog.

RICHARD. I'm lying on the basement floor of my parent's house at 4 am and I'm completely fucked up, all kinds of unbelievable shit jacking through me, and the phone rings, its Kathie, she's completely fucked up too, and bored, and she goes "wanna get married." So I'm like, okay, next thing I know we're in a cab on our way to the airport for a 6:30 flight to Vegas. And we're in the back of the cab tearing and clawing each other, screaming laughing, I've got her panties hanging from my ear…it was fucking epic.

But we get to the airport and we're at the terminal waiting for our flight, she's got this screeching grin stuck to her face like a postage stamp, I'm squinting from the glare and I start to feel this sour thing happen to my throat.

But we do it anyway. It isn't bad, at first. We still get fucked up, we still have fun. She's a lot more laid back than my first two wives. Then she starts in with "we need a dog, we NEED a dog, we gotta get one NOW" and her eyes are all twinkly and maternal, what the fuck do I care, a dog, great, love dogs, bring it on. No idea what I'm in for. Walking cleaning washing feeding fetching training picking up doody with paper towels in every fucking room because the damn animal thinks it's funny to watch me clean up its doody, and frankly I don't blame him but it's still a downright mean existence.

Then she tells me she's pregnant. I'm shocked, I mean I never used a thingie because you know we were married and I thought she had that all taken care of. She suddenly becomes this angry angry woman, she's angry at me every single day, it's incredible, and the dog becomes the centerpiece of our misery. I'm not taking care of him right, I'm not playing with him enough, I'm leaving the doody in the living room for too many days, and I'm thinking, what the fuck is gonna happen with a BABY?

TWO GUYS MOVING HEAVY STUFF

David Riedy

Bob, a sopping wet milquetoast who has always been second-dog to his friend Bill, finally has enough of Bill's griping about his girlfriend who has just thrown Bill out, again, and unleashes a uncharacteristic tirade.

BOB. What do you want me to say? She treats you like shit—she tells you you're pathetic, worthless, a non-human, uh, ape. And she's violent—she's always throwing things. I'm afraid to visit you because I might get hurt. I mean you still don't have a t.v. since she threw that one at you when you were sleeping that time. And you take it—you crawl back and beg for more! It's like you like it or something! You are totally fucked up over this woman. Like a piece of your brain broke off. Crystal says I should just stay out of it— that if you want to end up dead under some—big appliance I should let you—that you want to stay with this—this—bitch. She's a bitch, she is. And you know I don't use that word. Nobody likes her but you. I can't stand her. She—she's like, uh, some kind of happiness vampire—she sucks all the happiness out of anyone who comes near her. And you want to know what I think you should do? I think you should run as far away as fast as you can and never stop. You should be glad she threw you out of that crummy little apartment. She has given you a fucking gift by throwing you out! You should have a fucking party because that happiness-sucking vampire fucking bitch Linda has let you out of her grip!

(A moment of stunned silence.)

And I am not dancing again just because I said her name.

THE TYPOGRAPHER'S DREAM

Adam Bock

Dave, a court stenographer, when considering the kind of person best suited for court reporting, recalls how his high school typing class spurred a unique interest in his current occupation.

DAVE. Look. Court reporting isn't for everyone. Some people (*Pause.*) You start with typing. In high school maybe, you're all sitting, row after row after row of typewriters was the way it was when I got started, me here, Monalisa Garalletti next to me, Toby Moore behind me whispering, and you're typing asdf asdf asdf fdsa fdsa fdsa asdf asdf asdf fdsa fdsa fdsa and some people, well, that's enough to make them crazy, Monalisa, and they end up doing something with their feet instead of their hands like soccer or postal worker or waitressing, Monalisa, or something with their ears instead of their hands like phone operator or sound engineer. But, if you like it, you keep going and then it's "type the copy exactly as it is given below. Spell, space, begin and end each line, each paragraph, punctuate and capitalize precisely as shown. Make no erasures" and if that makes you crazy, well maybe you like doing things with your hands but you want to be less precise, and so you go and you work on an assemble line, or you work as a surgeon or you work as someone who replaces window panes, Toby. But, if you like it, you practice, you might do drills, like alphabetic drills, rhythm drills, alternate hand drills, you might make "most frequently used word lists" and then practice them and you get good. You get really good at it. And fast. Hundred and twenty words a minute junior in high school and people are looking at you. And people are mentioning it to you. And to each other. And. And you hear about court reporting and you think Hm. And then you find out. Court reporting. It's an entirely different world.

THE TYPOGRAPHER'S DREAM

Adam Bock

Dave, a court stenographer, realizes that he's lost his own voice in the process of recording what everyone else has to say.

DAVE. I started listening to myself. And I heard what she was talking about. *(Pause.)* And I thought about my work. How when you're a court reporter, you just capture and repeat what other people say and you're practically not even there. You're just neutral. *(Pause.)* How since I'm a court reporter, I'm neutral. And maybe I don't tell my own side of *(Pause.)* And it's hard it's a hard it's hard for me to I have a hard time, my tongue gets tripped up. And if you go just a, if I go just a little bit farther with it all, I can see that, when I've been talking like that, I've been putting myself over there, and it's as though I've been talking about someone else all the time, as if I've been talking about that person. Not about me, but about that "you" person. The whole time. So then. Where have I been? I guess that's. *(Pause.)* Where have I been? *(Pause.)* Where have I been? All this time? *(Pause.) (Exits.)*

THE UNSEEN

Craig Wright

Wallace, imprisoned by a totalitarian regime for unknown crimes, accuses a fellow prisoner of spying on him.

WALLACE. You could be hypnotized or programmed or somehow surgically altered, Mister Valdez, and you could be taking everything in that I say and do without even realizing it, and you could be painstakingly, unconsciously recording it in a secret sector of your brain hidden even from you, Mister Valdez—even from you. And then, when they take you to the room for treatment, they could activate that secret sector of your brain with a signatory word, for instance, or an electrode, or a pulsing electromagnetic device of some sort, and thus make you talk and divulge the contents of that secret sector of your brain that is hidden even from you, Mister Valdez—even from you. And then, once they'd extracted the information, they could close the doors once more, and darken the long cerebral hallways leading to that secret sector of your brain hidden even from you, Mister Valdez, even from you— and then they'd sweetly send you back here to continue sponging up the messy information that's continuously dripping from my mouth. In this manner, you could be a spy and you would not even know it.

THE UNSEEN

Craig Wright

Smash, a prison guard for a totalitarian regime, tells his prisoners about a man he has just tortured.

SMASH. Yes! *(After a beat:)* I started with the eyes. I slipped my thumbnails in past the corners and pushed. Felt them scrape past the backs of the sockets and out they came. Really easy. And I held them in my hands and looked at them. It was like my hands were staring up at me now, with all that misery, asking me what I'd just done. So I squished them to bits in my fists and they ran down my wrists and my arms like they'd never been anything but liquid. There was nothing but grease in my hands. And he's screaming. Begging for his mommy. Begging for his daddy. Begging and crying and, get this, *promising to be good.* I couldn't take it.

WOULD YOU PLEASE FUCKING SHUT THE FUCK UP?

I shoved two fingers deep down his throat, far back as my hand could go. So he's biting my wrist, you know? And I dug my nails down through his tongue, it was tough, but I pulled back his head as I did it to give myself leverage and then they popped through. I had blood spraying up in my face. And I pulled, and I pulled, like a hook, until it stretched and it tore out and his throat filled up with the blood. But he still kept on choking and screaming. So I went to the table and got the wrench and I pushed it all the way down his throat, you know, jammed it down through the vocal cords, down so hard that it straightened his throat and his head tilted back. But he wouldn't stop making, you know, sound! And his chest was pumping and there was piss and shit running out everywhere and his face was still twitching and crying, he wouldn't fucking stop!

I set him on fire. And I sat there and watched while he burned. For a while, he even kept moving in the flames, so I couldn't tell when he was, you know, flailing and when he was falling apart. I couldn't tell what mattered. But I watched until the fire went out and I was sitting across from this thing. In a room full of wet stone and smoke. And the faucet had never stopped running. *(After a beat:)* But the knowing—it never got better. The knowing only got worse. It got deeper and wider until now I'm wrapped up inside it like I'll never get out. It's forever.

(Brief pause.)

I never meant to be this kind of person.

THE VIRGIN MOLLY

Quincy Long

A male Marine Corps recruit has just given birth to a child in the Sexual Orientation and Evaluation Unit at a Marine Corps boot camp. The Civilian, both witness and guide to the event, speaks to the audience.

CIVILIAN. Okay
I'm in a bar one time
And this guy
Old guy
Throws a drink on me
I hit him
He hits me
The place is in a uproar
Cops come
Arrest me
Arrest him
Throw us in the paddy wagon
Handcuffed
Together
And on the way downtown he tries to get
Friendly
I'm not friendly
He throws up on my shoes
We get there
To the jail
Surprise
This guy's loaded
Money's no object
He goes my bail
We go to his place
What a place

Money money everywhere
Art
People
He takes me to his library
Shuts the door
All these books
I'm still up
Wanna dance
Party
Uh uh
He sits me down
All serious now
Wants to talk about the hard stuff
War stories about
Courage
Wisdom
Duty
Friendship
The helmet with the bullet hole in it
Love
This from a guy that pukes on my shoes
But
I'm listenin
Cause
I don't know
Everybody needs something

THE WAX

Kathleen Tolan

Ben, a gay theater critic, discusses the unusual way he met his current boyfriend and addresses the unfair prejudice that befalls a critic.

BEN. Anyway, you asked earlier how I'd met Hal. I was at one of the many incredibly strained soirees one is obliged to attend, the obligatory plastic cup of Chablis and obligatory vapid chat after an awards ceremony, and if you yourself were a judge, feigning delight in the recipient when more often than not the "artist" your committee has agreed on is rarely anyone's first choice—usually it's the least interesting, the least surprising or extreme, the one no one can get hot about in one direction or another. I had recently broken up with Chip and had disintegrated in the most typical and mundane manner, was on my forth or fifth Chablis and in any case was quite unhinged, and I recognized Hal, he was standing next to me, as a composer I had, actually, once, been quite excited by—. We began talking but then I saw him glance over to the door, looking for a way to make an escape, realizing who I was—you know, the hated critic. And I felt this surge of desperation, the need to somehow bridge the chasm—there it is, the chasm.

(Beat.)

And I grabbed his sleeve and said—and my voice I realized was shaking, I was weeping, I sort of screamed in this high pitched sort of wheeze—Why doesn't anyone write a play about a critic who is a person? I mean, we all have our judgments, we all have our opinions, we all say things, cutting, damning things—because we all have standards, values, ideals—we actually believe in something—and just because I do it in public, I put it out there for everyone to see, I'm either treated like a leper, like the lowest scum, or even, believe it or not, worse—like some tyrant king who requires to be surrounded by sycophants, who could never be seen as a person, a fellow person, no, that just could never be possible. Well, I may as well go sell shoes. Why don't I do that? I think I'll just go sell shoes. He looked at me like I was the insane person that I was and I realized there was nothing for me to do but make good on my threat—though given my profession one would've thought I could've come up with something a bit more damning, a bit more salacious, but this is what I spewed in my sodden state. I left, he followed, not, he told me later, out of any coherent interest, but rather a perverse curiosity. It was an afternoon, grey, wet, midtown, I weaved and lurched uptown past the theatre marquis, Carnegie Hall, Columbus Circle, Lincoln Center, occasionally glancing back to see that he was still following, wondering if I should stop and curse him out or just grab a cab and go home, wondering if in fact he was the sick one, what did he want from me? Then there I was, standing outside Harry's Shoes. I went in, sat down, my heart thumping. He came in, sat down next to me. We just sat there. Then a guy asked us what we wanted. He looked at me, very sweet, gave me a little smile, asked if I wanted anything. I said no. We left, went home together. We've been together ever since.

WHATEVER, WHENEVER

Jesse Kellerman

Reggie, a 40-something salesman, congratulates himself on a triumphant business deal.

REGGIE. I'm in town on business. They sent me out to close this deal with the veep of management. This company—I unfortunately cannot tell you *which* company, because that is protected information—but they were on the brink of dropping us, because our contract with them is coming up for negotiation. This is a big contract we have with them, understand?

This is not something we can afford to just flush down the fucking toilet, get it?

So I am getting nowhere with this guy in the board room. Pressure from the other veep, some prick with a mechanical pencil—pressure from this, pressure from that. And I am thinking I need to get this guy outta here, the veep I'm working on—I can't tell you his name, you see—

He's clearly the kind of fellow who likes to cut loose but *cannot*. In theory, yes, he would like to be out there on the weekends. But in practice: he cannot. He is surrounded by suits—he himself *is* a suit—but he does not *want* to be a suit. I thought, "We need to get this guy out of the office, and only *then* can I begin to get anywhere to salvage my firm's contract." I tell him, "Look, let's meet after work. In a more relaxed atmosphere, we can chat, man to man, et cetera." *(Smiling.)* You know where I took him?

Get this: I took him to a flesh house.

Strip joint. I found this place the last time I was in the city. He had no idea where I was taking him. But he went. You know why?

Because truly, secretly, that's what he wanted. *(Pause.)* Y'see, we are *always* attracted to that thing but cannot take it, because of *rules*, because the wife says no, because you have *responsibilities*... But when someone else is guiding you there, you'll run like a puppy. I took him. And then he was happy, just the way I wanted it. I got him right in the right place, the place *he himself* wanted to be. And then he was *mine! That* is the secret of business! You want a drink?